D1444055

FROM THE FILES OF SAVOY GRAVES

Adeline

MARK TORRES

INDIEOWL
PRESS

4700 Millenia Blvd
Ste 175 #90776
Orlando, FL 32839

info@indieowlpress.com
IndieOwlPress.com

ADELINE

Cover design by NightOwlFreelance.com
Cover art © Olivia Torres

Paperback ISBN-13: 978-1-949193-70-1
Hardcover ISBN-13: 978-1-949193-71-8

For my wife and children who complete me.

CONTENTS

Adeline

[signature]

Dear Margaret,
Enjoy the book!

[signature]

Red Bird

The clanging of heavy keys announced his approach. She knew that sound all too well. It had terrorized her soul for some time now. He entered the room, securing the door behind him. With enough wits to know not to resist him and a will that had long been broken, she stood near the bed with her back to the door, her head tilted up toward the small inaccessible window. He walked up behind her and lifted her hospital gown, grabbing her waist more tightly than usual. She tried not to focus on the sharp pain, even though it was all she could feel. The shame of being taken against her will had long been suppressed. At one time she thought their encounters were borne from love, but she lacked the capacity to understand sooner that it was anything but love.

He began his routine assault of her body. She remained frozen and obedient. Several beatings—some physical, most psychological, had taught her not to deviate from his unholy script. Hoping that it would all end sooner than usual, she tried to shift her focus, but the grimy white-tiled wall offered nothing but dark distant memories and hopeless malaise.

She had long questioned her fate...*Why am I here? Aren't I special? Is there something wrong with me?* Such self-contemplation only left her more drained. But it hadn't always been this way. Back in another lifetime, she had a zest for life. She greeted everyone with beaming eyes and the brightest smile and would always say, "I am Adeline Marie Deveraux. My friends call me Addy. You can call me Addy." Her gentle nature is the product of a genetic disposition rendering her unable to differentiate between friend and enemy, from safe and dangerous. This became more pronounced as she aged, and her body matured. Only the cruelest of ironies could see this young woman, with all her innocence, purity and freedom condemned for those same precious qualities.

A cardinal flying past the barred window caught her eye. She tilted her head to take in its brilliant red feathers, shining like a beacon against the radiant early morning sky. She had seen this red bird before. It was majestic, yet so lonely, she thought. She immediately identified with the divine creature, even though their worlds were separated by barred windows, stone walls, and boundless air. She had seen many birds flying outside of the window of her room at the Thornwood Manor Psychiatric Center in Rockland County, New York where she had resided since being committed in 1976. It had been her home for nearly two years now. It is a hell reserved for the most severely impaired. It is no place for one, like her, with a gentle, misunderstood soul.

A guttural grunt and the tightening of his hands signaled his crude finish. And then, in a demented attempt to connect with her, he told her to say his name. This had long been his twisted fetish. She would usually utter his name so that he would leave quickly. But today, she was not inclined to do so. Instead, she sat motionless with her head sunk low, praying for his departure. He placed a finger under her chin to lift her face and said, "Ah, come on, don't be that way." Stripped of all humanity, her body and soul had been defiled long enough, and today the perverse request to state his name triggered a spark of rebellion within her that had long been dormant. She'd had enough, and now, sitting up and focusing her gaze out the window, as if searching in vain for the pretty red bird, she opened her lips, and with a firm voice said, "My name is Adeline Marie Deveraux."

"Lower your voice," he barked and stepped back away from the bed while fastening his belt.

But she would not be deterred and spoke more loudly, more fiercely. "My name is Adeline Marie Deveraux. My friends call me Addy. You cannot call me Addy. You are a bad man. You hurt me."

"I said lower your voice, bitch," he hissed. She continued, "My name is Adeline Marie Deveraux. My friends call me Addy. You cannot call me Addy."

Desperate to silence her, he leaned in and wrapped his large hands around her swan-like neck.

She gasped for air, but continued with a strained voice, "You cannot call me Addy." She attempted to stand, but he held her firmly by the neck, forcing her to remain in a seated position on the bed. Barely audible, she repeated, "You…cannot…call…me…Addy."

His rage intensified.

She continued to repeat her words while feebly slapping and

3

scratching at his muscled arms.

He momentarily released his grip, reaching for a nearby pillow on the bed. Pressing the pillow over her face, he pushed her down onto her back on the bed and laid on top of her. Unable to breathe, her attempts to escape became weaker and weaker; her mind and body drifted toward the red bird.

The brute redoubled his efforts, pressing the pillow tighter and tighter until there was no more fight left in her. He felt her struggle diminish but waited another minute before releasing the pillow.

Adeline lay motionless, her lifeless eyes staring up toward the window. The cardinal circled back and, with a few rapid flaps of its wings, let out a loud chirp, before flying away from that cold place.

Home Sweet Home

Nestled just off the Cross Island Parkway, and adjacent to Belmont Park, lies the incorporated village of Floral Park, New York. Straddling the western border of Nassau County, Floral Park is home to approximately 16,000 residents. With its close proximity to New York City and boasting the small-town charm of a quiet suburban neighborhood, Floral Park is a natural draw for many families seeking to plant their roots. Indeed, Floral Park lives up to the town's motto which is simply, "A Wonderful Place to Live."

Formerly called East Hinsdale, Floral Park was once the westernmost fringe of the Hempstead Indians territory, until farmers inhabited the area and began to settle. In 1874, John Louis Childs settled in the area and purchased much of the land to begin a local business in the horticulture industry, selling seeds and bulbs for flowers. Over the years, Childs' prominence in business and politics grew. Later, with the arrival of the Post Office and the Long Island Railroad, many of the streets were named after flora and the town's name of Floral Park was adopted.

With the expected birth of their first child, Savoy Graves and his wife Lola settled in Floral Park to plant their roots together. The couple chose a modest three-bedroom cape on a sleepy block adjacent to the outer fringes of the omnipresent Belmont Park. They both adore the town; although Lola, forever the history buff, occasionally laments that the town should do more to celebrate its deep history. Fortunately, the home boasts a large backyard, perfectly suited for Clubber, their lumbering golden retriever and Vito, his diminutive counterpart Yorkshire terrier. The couple has been living comfortably with Savoy juggling his successful law practice, along with investigating a select few unsolved murder cases. Most recently, he'd worked on a case involving the death of Lola's mother.

On this warm spring day, Savoy and Lola were playing fetch with the dogs when the telephone rang. Lola entered from outside, answered and said, "Yes, just a moment please." She called out to Savoy, telling him he had a call. Clubber came rushing back with a tennis ball in his mouth and placed it at his feet. Savoy tossed the ball deep into the back of the yard and jogged over to take the call.

"Good afternoon. Are you the same Savoy Graves that worked on the Maria Cruz murder case?" asked an elderly woman with a raspy voice.

A bit surprised at being identified in such a manner, Savoy replied, "Yes, I am. Who is this?"

"Mr. Graves, my name is Loretta Deveraux. I read about your

efforts in that case and would like to discuss retaining your services to investigate the death of my daughter in 1977. Would you be able to meet me at my home? I hate to impose upon you, but I am quite elderly, and due to my failing health, it is too difficult for me to leave my home."

Looking out the window, Savoy was distracted by the sight of his pregnant wife, Lola, tossing the tennis ball for Clubber to retrieve while holding Vito who was yapping playfully.

Sensing his distraction, Ms. Deveraux said, "Mr. Graves. I am a woman with modest resources, but I assure you that I can pay you for your services."

Savoy replied, "Ms. Deveraux, I don't choose cases for the money. I select cases when justice has been heinously deni—"

"Mr. Graves, this is precisely why I have called you. I assure you that my situation will fit squarely within your...criteria. All I ask is that you give me one hour of your time. And if you are not interested in what I have to tell you, then you can simply leave, and I will never bother you again. Can you do that for me? Please?"

Lola tossed the ball again and looked in his direction, offering a wide smile. "Sure, Ms. Deveraux," he replied. "I apologize. I didn't mean to sound insensitive. I just have a lot on my plate right now. I will be glad to meet with you and discuss your situation.

"Thank you, Mr. Graves," she replied.

Savoy reached for a pen and paper and jotted down her address. "That isn't too far from the Tappan Zee Bridge, right?"

"Yes," she replied, then thanked him and wished him a good day.

Savoy returned to the yard, and Clubber playfully sprinted toward him with the tennis ball tucked in his mouth.

"Who was that?" asked Lola.

"I don't quite know," he replied. "A prospective client I suppose. She lives up in Westchester and wants me to look into her daughter's death in 1977. I can't shake that feeling, though."

"What feeling?" replied Lola. "The same feeling I had when I first read the newspaper article about your mother's death." Savoy shook his head and said, "Come on. Let's go inside and have lunch. Besides, you should rest."

She smiled. "Me? Rest? Husband, this baby I am carrying is baby-lite and we still have many months to go until the big day. If anyone needs rest, it's you. I can tell because you have that look in your eye again."

"That look?" Savoy asked with a wide grin.

"Yes," she replied. "The same kind of look you had when we met. Focused, dialed-in, like you're thinking a thousand miles ahead. It looks like the detective in you is churning again."

"Well, that detective may not be alone this time," Savoy replied.

Lola looked on quizzically as he continued.

"If you're up to it, why don't you join me?" he asked.

"Join you?" she said. "Really?"

"Sure," he replied. "It would be great to spend some time together. Besides, if they ever make a movie about our encounters, just imagine the stars they'd choose to play our parts."

Savoy smiled as he took Lola by the hand and the two walked toward the house. Savoy looked down at Clubber. His almond-brown eyes remained fixated on the tennis ball in his hand in anticipation of another toss while Vito anxiously awaited behind him, hoping to get a head start. Happy to oblige, Savoy reared his arm back and tossed it deep into the yard, sending both dogs racing for it. As they headed inside, Savoy was consumed with curiosity at the identity of Loretta

Deveraux and the death of her daughter. As always, Lola was right. His detective's mind was already churning.

Steely Resolve

By all accounts, Bonnie Beacham was a rare success story in her line of work. A full-time position as a forensic pathologist in the Medical Examiner's office in Rockland County did not come along very often, and when it did, it certainly wasn't a position offered to many women in the 1970s.

Born in Farmingville, New York, Bonnie was raised by proud middle-class parents. She was the youngest of three sisters, and nothing came easy for her family. Her mother had died of leukemia while she was quite young, and she was forced to fend for herself, which was challenging given her diminutive size. Yet what Bonnie lacked in physical stature, she certainly made up for in sheer will. Dubbed "Mighty Mouse" by her friends, Bonnie was as tough as she was loyal.

She had also always been an excellent student—a trait borne of loyalty to her father who had promised to give her everything he could in life if she kept her grades up. Thus, when it came to her academics, Bonnie did not disappoint. She finished at the top of her class each year and was in the running for valedictorian in her senior year of high school.

Bonnie's search for college was short. She knew exactly what she wanted and where she wanted to attend college, and when she received an acceptance letter from the prestigious Columbia University, accompanied by a full scholarship, her course was set. Bonnie earned a Bachelor of Science degree, and then enrolled in the school's medical program. While there, Bonnie met many students from all walks of life. Yet, despite their differences, most had the singular goal of becoming a doctor. Certainly, given the cost and time it would take to complete medical school, residencies and further training, becoming a doctor seemed to be the only logical conclusion. But Bonnie had other plans. For as long as she could remember, her goal was to become a Forensic Pathologist. Of course, Bonnie was aware that this was a far less glamorous career and would certainly not generate the income that being a doctor would. She was also warned that her chosen field was rife with political corruption and misogyny. Despite the dismal career prospects, she forged ahead

Bonnie completed eight years of pre-medical and then medical school at Columbia before undergoing an intensive residency program at New York University Medical Center where she received supervised training in anatomical, clinical, and surgical pathology. There she learned how to examine, recognize, and interpret diseases and causes of death in physical specimens. Bonnie spent many sleepless nights fearing that she could not keep up with the rigorous program. She knew that she could have easily foregone the struggles and settled on becoming a doctor where she would earn a far higher income, but the promise she had made to her father—of reaching her full potential, kept her going.

Bonnie remained steadfast and finally completed the program, and after a grueling round of final examinations, she became a Board-certified, licensed physician in anatomical, clinical and surgical pathology. She was among a mere dozen other candidates to complete the same feat. One year later, Bonnie applied for and was accepted by the Rockland County Medical Examiner's Office; a position she had proudly held for the last two years.

As she sat in her office finishing up some paperwork on a recent case, the phone rang. "Good morning, this is the Rockland County ME Office, Bonnie Beacham speaking," she said.

"Ms. Beacham," said one of the attendants from the nearby Thornwood Manor Psychiatric Center. "We need someone to come here right away. There's been a fatality. It was discovered this morning."

"Did you notify the local police?" Bonnie calmly asked.

"Yes," replied the woman. "Authorities are on the way and they asked that we relay this information to your office as well."

Unfortunately, Bonnie's office had received a fair amount of calls over the years from Thornwood Manor. The varied health status of patients, coupled with the dramatic treatment for mental illness with little to no proper oversight in such an unforgiving environment, occasionally produced gruesome results, including patient suicides or other deaths. Bonnie asked where the body was found.

The attendant replied, "The patient was discovered inside a room in the Bradley Building: the young women's ward. Adeline Marie Deveraux, 19-year-old female. It appears to have been a suicide by hanging."

Bonnie jotted the date and time of the call in her log book: April 15, 1977; 9:39 a.m., followed by other pertinent information relayed to her. She then told the attendant, "We will be there as soon as possible. Please be sure that the room is secured. Do I make myself clear?"

The woman replied yes before ending the call.

Bonnie teemed with anticipation. She always did when a new call came in. It enabled her to put her skills into action; a skill that was borne from the lengthy and grueling education she had spent many years to receive. Bonnie had always believed that some examiners were lazy, that they didn't dig deep enough into their cases. Not that she ever thought that any of them would shirk their duty. Their Hippocratic Oath, ethical commitments, and professional training would never allow them to, but to her, some in her field would never dig deep enough. To Bonnie, each body that entered her office had a story to tell; some were quite easy to read, others more secretive. At times, either on a hunch or by exploring a far-fetched theory, she would feel compelled to venture deeper into some cases. This would often put her at odds with her supervisor, Chief Medical Examiner, Martin Walcott, who often chastised Bonnie for pushing the limits of the department's precious, and limited, resources. As much as she'd tried to conform, her steely resolve and relentless pursuit for the truth persisted. Bonnie Beacham simply could not operate any differently.

With information about a new death at Thornwood Manor, Bonnie sprinted down the hall to relay it to Walcott. She did not know it at the time, but her life was about to change forever.

Fragility

Originally diagnosed in the early 1960's, Ohr's Syndrome is a rare genetic disorder that occurs once in about 10,000 births. This genetic, multisystem disorder is caused by a random deletion of chromosomes. The inherent social, physical, and intellectual challenges make it very difficult for those with Ohr's Syndrome to maintain an independent livelihood. Another serious concern, particularly among children, is the tendency of OS patients to be overly friendly, or more commonly referred to as an inability to understand the concept of "stranger danger."

Even though there is no cure, medical science has come a long way in treating those who have Ohr's Syndrome. Today, the only way to definitively test for OS is a specialized blood test. However, back in the early 1960s through the 70s, the condition was poorly diagnosed and there was little funding toward understanding it.

Adeline Marie Deveraux was born on June 3, 1956. Although doctors didn't know it at the time, she was born with Ohr's Syndrome. Thus, they were confounded by her symptoms and unable to provide adequate medical treatment. Difficulties arose when in her mid-teens Adeline's body began to develop as her cognitive abilities lagged. This left her overbearing father, Steven Deveraux, forever fearful that wayward men would take advantage of her. His paranoia drove a wedge between him and his wife, Loretta, about how to properly raise their daughter. Loretta believed in her heart that, although delicate and somewhat vulnerable, Adeline was an angel who could thrive in a loving and stable home. Unfortunately, Steven was unable to escape his paranoid delusions, which led him to make other plans.

The King

Savoy and Lola were blessed to live in a town with many friendly neighbors, but for them none were more reliable than Stanley Korman. Stanley was born and raised in Floral Park. After a brief stint in the army, he returned and, at the urging of his father, joined a trade school to learn the art of welding. Once completed, Stanley became an apprentice in one of the most powerful labor unions in New York. Over the years he became a master welder and worked for many years before retiring with a modest pension to live in the same house where he was raised.

Stanley is as tough as they come. Despite nearing 70 years of age, his large 6' 5" inch frame with massive shoulders and overly large hands always commanded respect. In his youth, Stanley was an avid athlete who excelled in all sports. He was even a professional roller derby player at the height of that sport's popularity. It was there that he met his future wife, Dorothy, who played the sport as well. The two were nicknamed the roller derby "King" and "Queen" until their joint retirement which culminated in the retiring of their numbers; his infamous number 4 and her celebrated, albeit odd, number 67.

Stanley and Dorothy had two children, a boy and a girl. Their son, Stanley Jr., died at a young age in a horrific motorcycle accident. It was a most tragic event that occurred on a rainy night at a popular drag racing strip in Queens, New York. The couple, who would never recover from the loss of Stanley Jr., poured all their love into their daughter, Charlotte, who lived at the home until going off to college on the west coast.

The couple lived alone for several years until Dorothy passed away after suffering a massive heart attack. After Dorothy's death, Charlotte became estranged from her father, which left Stanley to live alone in the family home. Years of backbreaking work in hazardous conditions, culminated to the onset of a minor brain aneurism believed to have been caused by many years of inhaling excessive welding smoke, along with his long history of playing physically demanding sports, had taken a toll on his body. Although, nowadays, Stanley walks with a steady limp, he remains a strong and independent man.

Stanley immediately embraced Savoy and Lola. In some ways, his neighbors reminded him of him and his wife in their younger years. He first met with the couple after asking Savoy to review some legal documents pertaining to a lawsuit he had filed against a welding company he'd formerly worked for. Savoy was glad to help his burly neighbor who was mutually helpful in assisting with minor home repairs in and around the couple's home. The three would often dine together and engaged in many discussions about life and family. Stanley would regale them with stories of his military service, his lengthy work experience, and, of course, roller derby. He often lamented about not remaining in regular contact with his daughter, Charlotte, who lives in Nevada and is a sky-dive trainer and enthusiast. Despite Lola's repeated efforts, she can never convince him to call her. His usual response is, "She's probably too busy."

Since he lives alone, Stanley relished the opportunity to take care of Clubber and Vito when the couple travelled. He even let the dogs have the run of the house, often spoiling them rotten. So, when Savoy asked if he could watch the dogs while they investigate this new case, Stanley was more than happy to oblige. "Take as long as you need," he replied with a smile. "Just remember, table scraps are on the menu."

Savoy smiled back and thanked him for his help.

Cover

The man stared with wild eyes at Adeline's lifeless body. He felt some regret, but mostly frustration. He would have preferred to continue having his way with her, but she wouldn't keep quiet and had to be silenced, lest he be exposed. But in taking her life, he now had a new problem. The body of a dead woman on the grounds would surely trigger a thorough investigation. He had to think fast. He realized that if her death was made to look like a suicide, a somewhat common fate in a place like this, then his cover may be protected. He was exhausted but had to act quickly. The entire floor would soon be bustling with the incoming morning staff.

He wiped his mouth with the back of his hand before quietly sliding the bed under the barred window. He then removed a length of rope several feet long that he always kept handy. He stood on the bed to secure one end of the rope around the bars of the window leaving the other end dangling near the floor. He then lifted Adeline's body. Although her frame was demure, the weight of her lifeless body caused him to struggle more mightily than he expected. He held up her body in a standing position on the bed and tightened the other end of the rope around her neck so that her body would eventually hang from the rope to simulate a suicide by hanging. He did this several times until her feet were approximately 18 inches off the ground. He tugged on each end of the rope to ensure its sturdiness. It held just fine. Then he slid the bed back to its original location.

As he began to gather his belongings, he caught a glimpse of Adeline's lifeless eyes peering at and seemingly through him. He paused for a moment and then gently closed her eye lids. Satisfied with his macabre stagecraft, he slipped out of the room as quietly as he'd entered it.

Tarrytown

Approximately 30 miles north of New York City on the eastern shore of the Hudson River, is Tarrytown, a vibrant hamlet in Westchester County that is rich in history. Originally inhabited by the native Weckquasgeek tribe, the Dutch began to settle in the area in 1645 and made a living from farming, fur trapping, and fishing. Due to the unique mineral-rich soil, the area saw tremendous growth from harvesting wheat products. In 1681, a wealthy businessman named Frederick Philipse bought a great amount of acreage in the area and constructed several wheat mills, which, for most of the 18th century, dominated the economic success of the area.

During the Revolutionary War, Major John Andre, a co-conspirator of Benedict Arnold, was arrested in Tarrytown, convicted and hanged for his crimes. In 1820, Washington Irving's release of The Legend of Sleepy Hollow referenced the area of Tarry Town. The area was the home of John D. Rockefeller, whose famous mansion Kykuit was erected in 1906—later the site of numerous labor-related riots. Tarrytown was also the site of the General Motors car manufacturing plant until its closure in 1996.

In 1955, the Tappan Zee Bridge was erected over the Hudson River, connecting Westchester and Rockland Counties. Today, Tarrytown and its sister town, Sleepy Hollow—originally named North Tarrytown— celebrate a rich history with numerous landmarks and a shared school district, set among the bucolic rolling hills and peaceful small-town life near the Hudson River. The Deveraux family has made Tarrytown their home for several generations.

As they made their way along the Palisades Parkway to the Deveraux home, Savoy was consumed with that all-too familiar mixture of anticipation and skepticism. He was on yet another journey; an unknown mission—the likes of which may have a profound impact on his life. He glanced at Lola who was rummaging through her bag to see if she had brought cell phone chargers and other necessary items. Her company was the reason for his optimism. The once self-proclaimed "little detective" was not so little anymore, and even better, he was no longer alone.

Savoy was emboldened by having Lola by his side. The horrifying details inherent in the type of investigation they were embarking on takes a very heavy physical and emotional toll, often leading to dark places. Lola, who has the uncanny ability to always see the good in everything, will help to quell that mental exhaustion. With his intelligent, strong willed and rational wife by his side, they can better assess their findings and lift each other up to cope with the emotional strain.

The drive over the Tappan Zee Bridge provided no shortage of majestic views in all directions. They exited onto a main road lined with boutiques, eateries, and a variety of stores serving every possible need. They saw a music store, a large theater, and a hardware store with random items such as wheel barrows and barbecues displayed out front. Their GPS guided them off the main road and up some steep and narrow streets toward a sleepy block, then to Loretta Deveraux's home at the end of the block.

Savoy and Lola exited the car and paused to take in the breathtaking features of the large yellow and brown two-story Victorian home. Although the home appeared to be very old and quite weathered, there was no mistaking its charm. The house boasted a tower with a witch's cap, several gables, and flashed glass on the many windows: all prominent features of a home built in that era.

The front entrance had an arbor in the center of a four-foot-high stone fence wrapping around the entire property. The couple walked through the arbor along a long cobblestone pathway toward the front of the home, adorned with a wide staircase, leading to a massive wraparound porch. Two crows perched on the rooftop and cawed loudly as they climbed the stairs to ring the bell. A young woman opened the door. She greeted them warmly, introduced herself as a home health care worker and led them into the home to meet their host.

Loretta Deveraux, a slender elderly woman in poor health and bound to a wheelchair, wore a red and white head scarf, covering what appeared to be a loss of her hair, no doubt from the cancer treatment she had been forced to endure. She fidgeted delicately in her wheelchair near a large window at the rear of the house overlooking a magnificent wooded backyard. She greeted them with a warm smile and said, "Please, have a seat." Still smiling, Loretta looked toward Lola, placed her hand on her heart and said, "This lovely woman must be Lola. I recognize you from the pictures in the newspaper. My deepest condolences concerning your mother."

"Thank you," replied Lola with a genuine smile.

"And, Mr. Graves. I am honored to meet you," said Loretta.

"The pleasure is all mine," he replied, reaching out to shake her warm, delicate hand. Looking back at Lola with a somber expression, Loretta said, "I pray that your husband can help me as he helped you."

"I will do my best, Ms. Deveraux," Savoy replied. "My wife will be joining me in this case."

A small photo album was placed on the table alongside a pot of coffee with several pastries. "Please," said Loretta, "help yourselves."

"This is a lovely home you have here, Ms. Deveraux," said Lola.

Loretta shook her head and held her hand up and replied "Call me Loretta and thank you. It requires a great amount of upkeep, but it is certainly home."

Savoy and Lola nodded politely.

Loretta continued, "Thank you for coming today. I understand that you are pressed for time." She cleared her throat.

"Mr. Graves, a few months ago, I received the most unfortunate news that I have late stage cancer. I am tired. I am beaten down and don't have much fight left. This disease has eaten my body, and chemotherapy has zapped all my zest for life. Quite frankly, I am ready for the good Lord to receive me. But before I draw my last breath, I have one wish—a wish that for far too long has eluded me. In fact, it is a wish that I have wasted a large portion of my life trying to ignore, mainly because I never thought it was attainable. Hell, part of me still didn't believe it was attainable until I read an article about your efforts in the Maria Cruz murder." She glanced at Lola sorrowfully before continuing. "Mr. Graves, what you did, when seemingly no one else would even try, inspired and revived me in a way that no dosage of chemotherapy or prayer has done before. Mr. Graves, as I've said, I am dying and do not have much time. With that said, I have a challenge for you. I would like to ask you to investigate the death of my daughter, Adeline Marie Deveraux."

Savoy glanced at Lola and then returned his gaze to Loretta.

She continued, "Let me tell you about my Adeline. She was our only child. You see, when I was pregnant with her, I knew in my heart that Adeline would be an angel and I was right. She was born crying but then our eyes met and she stopped to look at me. Our connection was immediate and unmistakable. She had this little upturned nose I called my "button" nose. I would often press upon it gently and it always brought a smile to her face."

Loretta explained that Adeline was a delicate child, later diagnosed with a mysterious genetic disorder. "She had what they call "Ohrs Syndrome." A rare genetic disorder that causes a great deal of physical, emotional, and intellectual disabilities. She was fairly high functioning for someone with that condition, which sort of masked her symptoms, but we had concerns about her ability to live a normal life. She was intelligent and could read quite well, but at the same time, she was unable to tie her shoes, tell time, or understand the value of money. One of our deepest worries was her inability to differentiate friends from strangers. This became more pronounced as she began to mature. My husband…"

Loretta paused to cough into a tissue she held with trembling hands before continuing. "My husband was a simple, but difficult, man, and he was not equipped with the patience that the parent of a special needs child requires. Do not let the size of this home fool you. We are of modest means; the house was gifted to us by my late parents. So, we could not afford the medical care that Adeline required. Even if we did, there weren't too many doctors at the time who understood or knew how to treat patients with Ohr's Syndrome. I devoted my life to raising our daughter, until I suffered a terrible accident here in our home that left me bound to this wheelchair. My husband worked long hours and was ill-equipped to assist in a meaningful way. You see, he was a drinker, a bad one, too, and he often flew into a rage when we discussed how to best care for our daughter. This rage intensified as Adeline matured, and the thought of Adeline being taken advantage of was too much for him to bear."

Loretta wiped some tears from her eyes with a handkerchief as Savoy glanced at the picture album on the table. On the cover, he could see a dark-haired young girl with a wide smile. Loretta continued, "I would like to blame my husband for our decision, but truth be told, I was too weak to resist his fits of rage and too ill to carry on without him. Perhaps, I too felt that we could never have provided our daughter with the upbringing that she needed. So, one evening, he came home from work with a brochure from Thornwood Manor Psychiatric Center. It was a place just across the river. He was carrying on for weeks about how it would offer Adeline a gentle place to receive the treatment she needed, the treatment that we could not have provided. Deep down, I could not bear to part with my sweet Addy, but given my physical condition, and his unwillingness to assist, I knew that it made practical sense. Not long after, we had our daughter committed into Thornwood Manor, and that decision has been my cross to bear ever since."

Loretta explained the process, with excruciating detail, the day that

Adeline, at the tender age of 18, was committed to Thornwood Manor. "Once there, we visited her as often as we could, but the time between each visit grew further and further. It became too physically demanding for me to visit, and it appeared that she was well cared for. Even though Thornwood began to slowly develop a negative reputation, we kept reassuring ourselves that we had made the right decision."

Savoy and Lola remained riveted as Loretta continued. "Adeline wrote beautiful letters to us, at first on a weekly basis. Then the letters were sent less and less," she lamented. "Weeks eventually turned into months, and time continued to pass us by. My husband and I were never able to have any other children, so her absence weighed heavy in our home. Then, one day—no, not one day, it was precisely April 15, 1977, I was in the garden and I received a call from Thornwood. I expected it to be Adeline, as sometimes she would call and we would talk for a bit, but it wasn't. The voice on the telephone was a nurse. She had called to tell me that my baby was dead. Loretta paused as tears welled up in her eyes. She looked away momentarily before continuing, "They found her hanging in her room. The coroner's report officially ruled it a suicide. Mr. Graves, Adeline was delicate and had her issues, but I tell you that she was generally healthy, and she certainly was never capable of committing suicide."

Savoy looked at Lola and took a deep breath. They both sat, as expecting parents, listening intently to Loretta describing, with such vivid and horrible detail, the painful decision she and her husband had made only to learn that Adeline would later die in that facility. Savoy wasn't prepared for such pain. Still, he was keenly aware that he needed more information if he had any chance of helping her. He cleared his throat and carefully choose his next words. "Loretta, I am sorry, but I have to ask you a personal question." The woman stared at him, in anticipation. "You said that your daughter entered Thornwood Manor at age 18 and was found dead a short time later."

She nodded with tear-filled eyes. "You also said that she was in despair at being admitted there. Forgive me for asking, but why do you believe that it wasn't a suicide?"

Loretta wiped the tears from her eyes and replied, "Mr. Graves, do you have children?" Savoy shook his head no, looked at Lola and said, "But we are expecting."

Loretta locked eyes with Lola and continued, "A mother knows her child. Adeline was a gentle soul. She would never hurt a fly, let alone herself. Whenever she was sick or hurt, she would dwell and even obsess about it for days. Such self-pity was another symptom of her condition. Am I really supposed to believe that she made a noose, fastened it around a barred window and hung herself?" Never. She couldn't even tie her shoes!

Savoy and Lola looked on. Sensing their speculation, Loretta asked him to go to a table at the end of the room and fetch a folder she had made for him. "In this folder there are copies of a few of her letters. Please read them. You will find a sensitive girl, but hardly broken. She simply lacked the ability to understand the wretched place she was in. Even we didn't fully appreciate how bad it was until years later." Savoy sifted through the letters. Poor handwriting made it difficult to read as the words were crunched too closely to each other.

"I realize they're hard to decipher. She had difficulty in manipulating writing instruments which led to her very poor handwriting," said Loretta.

Within the file was a page marked "Incident Report" written on letterhead from Thornwood Manor. Savoy carefully studied the document.

Loretta explained, "During her time there, Adeline befriended Elena Gonzalez, an orderly from Thornwood. She is very nice and periodically wrote us about Adeline's status. We still hear from her. Every year on Adeline's birthday, she sends us a comforting card. Her address is also in the folder. I believe it would be helpful to speak with the person who was closest to our daughter before her death." Savoy noted Elena's address in the Bronx as Loretta continued. "One day, Elena secretly sent us a copy of this report. We were told that a staff worker was reportedly bothering Adeline and we demanded answers. Apparently, he was spending an inordinate amount of time in and around the young woman's ward where Adeline resided. Elena told us that one day he was spotted leaning very close to Adeline who had her back against a fence outside one of the buildings. He must have sensed Adeline's vulnerability. The date of that incident was a few months before she was found dead."

Savoy studied the document. "Did this employee have a name?"

"That's the thing," Loretta replied. "They never gave us his name. They simply told us that he was reprimanded, and we never heard anything about it again. We had no reason to believe that it had continued or worsened."

Savoy studied Loretta carefully. Her facial expressions and reserved bodily movements revealed an immeasurable amount of grief, immediately invoking within him a great amount of pity for her. He was ill-prepared to address such grief, and when her eyes met his, he quickly shifted his gaze to the file which contained a copy of the police report, Adeline's death certificate, and the autopsy report.

Lola then asked, "Loretta, your husband, is he at home?"

"No" she solemnly replied. "Soon after the death of our daughter, he crawled into a bottle of booze and never came out of it. He kept on until one night he took his own life. He could never forgive himself for having Addy committed. As for me, I don't know how I will be judged by my maker, but as long as I have breath, I want to do all that can be done to find out the truth. I know in my heart that my little button did not kill herself. She couldn't have."

Savoy grappled with skepticism. Adeline was a mentally disabled young woman despondent about being committed into a strange and frightening psychiatric facility. Absent any evidence to the contrary, suicide seems like a plausible outcome. However, he has long learned to suspend all doubts until he had a chance to investigate. He also fought back against the urge to judge the Deveraux family on their decision to have their daughter committed in the first place. Families face crises all the time and unless he was truly in their shoes, he could never be certain how he would have handled it.

Lola continued asking Loretta more questions about Thornwood Manor as Savoy studied the woman. She possessed a sharp mind that seemed to offset her feeble physical demeanor with a body being decimated by cancer and confined to a wheelchair. Perhaps most striking to him were her dark hazel eyes, projecting an incredibly deep level of pain. Yet, through that pain, Loretta spoke with a fiery passion in defiance of the notion that her daughter died by her own hand. She also appeared to have accepted a certain level of responsibility for what happened to her daughter. With that, Savoy both respected and pitied her. Most importantly, he believed in her conviction, even if there was nothing that, at the moment, could support that belief. Nevertheless, Savoy knew that, regardless of the outcome, he would remain committed to doing everything he could to find out what happened to the young Adeline Marie Deveraux.

After a lengthy discussion, Savoy and Lola rose to thank Loretta for the information and hospitality. "We will check in with you periodically. I promise," said Savoy. The couple exited the home, and as they reached the bottom of the steps, Savoy looked up to the sky. Gone were the crows; he now spotted a cardinal flying above, its vivid red feathers shining brightly in the blue sky. It perched on a tree branch and began to sing loudly.

Recluse

Barry Gribbon has been a journeyman engineer in and around Rockland and Westchester counties for many years. By most accounts he is an average maintenance mechanic, even though his grimy appearance made him appear much more mechanically inclined than he really was. He first tried his hand in several permanent jobs with stable employers but was quickly and repeatedly rooted out for poor workmanship and a complete unwillingness to refine his professional skills. For the last few years, Barry had been working for local sub-contractor companies servicing a variety of heating and cooling equipment. The work was less stable and back-breaking, but it paid the bills.

Raised in a middle-class family in Newburgh, New York, Barry never really fit it. Even as a child, he was burdened with an ogre-like appearance and poor hygiene. He never excelled in sports, and he loathed any extracurricular activities. This naturally led to a solitary childhood and, as he aged, Barry became increasingly reclusive. After graduating from high school, with few other options, he entered a local trade school to learn the necessary skills to work in the heating and cooling industry. This, of course, was at the insistence of his abusive father who often said, "A man who doesn't have a trade, isn't a man."

In adulthood, Barry continued to live a solitary life. He never married nor had children. When he wasn't working at his various jobs, he occasionally spent his nights with local prostitutes who reluctantly indulged him in his ever-increasing perverse fantasies. Barry kept a large cache of pornography which he viewed regularly. His material migrated from soft pornography to more sadistic and violent material, including scenes where young female victims were filmed being raped and tortured.

Over time, Barry amassed a criminal record for a variety of crimes, ranging from drug possession to solicitation of prostitution. He once served a one-year sentence in Sing-Sing prison in Westchester for violent sexual behavior after he'd attempted to recreate the sadistic acts of his pornographic movies with a female escort. As a result, his criminal record has had an adverse impact on his current and prospective employment, but on each occasion, Barry would simply move on to work with one of the many other area contractors—after lying on his job application about his criminal record.

On this day, Barry sat in his one-bedroom apartment in Tuckahoe, New York suffering from a bad hangover after a night of drinking while watching game 7 of the 1975 World Series between the Cincinnati

Reds and the Boston Red Sox. Barry has long been a gambler and he bet heavily on the game. Unfortunately for him, the Reds won the game 4-3. He counted on his winnings to help cushion the blow from losing another job earlier in the week. The company he had worked for just hired a new human resources director who took it upon herself to delve into employee background checks. Once it was discovered that Barry had lied on his application, he was fired.

Seated at his large coffee-stained kitchen table, littered with empty beer cans and a full ashtray, Barry reflected on his life, aware that he could not continue down this path. He was no longer a young man, and the prospect of pursuing the same dead-end contractor jobs that offered little pay, meager benefits, and backbreaking work was not a stable plan. Working for contractors is young man's work, he thought. Barry's dilemma was daunting. Sooner or later his physical strength would begin to fail. He needed to find a stable and more suitable work environment, but with a criminal record, his options were dramatically dwindling.

He reached for a cold beer from the refrigerator, opened it and took a long swig. He closed the refrigerator door and saw a picture of his father held onto the door by a corkscrew magnet. He fought hard to drown out the voice of his disapproving father. He returned to the table determined to find something. After a thorough search of the local newspapers, Barry was pleased to see an advertisement for a mechanic's position at the nearby Thornwood Manor. The pay was average, and the job provided decent benefits, but most of all, it was an in-house job at a stable facility. This is precisely what he needed. Barry picked up the phone and with clumsy fingers, dialed the number to ask for instructions on how to apply. A young woman with a raspy voice answered the phone and explained the application process. Barry jotted down the details onto a used napkin and thanked the kind woman. Satisfied with his efforts, he chugged the rest of his beer and let out a loud burp. He then went to the living room and popped in his newest porn movie into his VCR—a sadistic tale with mild violence—and began to gratify himself.

Thornwood Manor

The Rockland County Historical Coalition of was founded in the late 1940s. Under the direction of local historians, and some very dependable volunteers, the non-profit group has strived for years to preserve the history of the numerous towns in the surrounding area. The group has always operated with a small budget, mostly from donations of local residents. These days, the group maintains a small, but valuable, collection of historical items from the area and members volunteer twice a week, usually in local libraries, answering queries from amateur historians and students writing historical essays.

Savoy and Lola had made an appointment to meet at the library in Stony Point, New York with the group's current historian, Ruth Metzger. Ruth is a retired history professor at New York University.

She volunteers her time at local historical societies, preserving and promoting the history of Rockland and Westchester counties. When they entered the library, Ruth greeted them with a warm smile. She was eager to meet them after they had contacted the group searching for information on Thornwood Manor.

Ruth escorted them to a room in the rear of the building. They sat at a small wooden table in the brightly-lit room. "I understand you are seeking information on Thornwood Manor," said Ruth.

Savoy and Lola each nodded as she continued.

"Well, let me first give you some background information based upon what we know about the facility from our archives." Ruth explained that the Thornwood Manor Psychiatric Center was built in 1901 in a small hamlet in Rockland County, approximately 75 miles outside of New York City. Named for the renowned psychiatrist Jozef Thornwood, the facility was touted as a model institution for the treatment and care of the mentally disabled and was intended to serve as a viable alternative to the overcrowded facilities in and around New York City. "Thornwood Manor was unlike most facilities of its time. It truly was a self-contained city."

Savoy and Lola listened intently as Ruth explained that the sprawling complex consisted of over 140 stone buildings, scattered over two-thousand acres of bucolic country and was separated by a steady creek, which meandered throughout the entire property not far from the majestic Hudson River. To maximize a therapeutic effect for patients, Thornwood was carefully designed to mimic home-style residences modelled after Virginia plantation homes. The patients were carefully separated by gender and the severity of their mental illness. Each building was no greater than three stories high, set no less than 25 yards apart and, to avoid overcrowding, each designed to house a maximum of 40 patients.

"As I have stated," said Ruth, "Thornwood had become a virtual self-contained city with its own food production, power and heat generation, laundry facilities, and so on. It also boasted its own railway, a fire department, sewage plants, staff and family housing, a school *and* a church. At its peak capacity, the Village housed nearly 5,000 patients."

Ruth further explained that the initial treatment for patients at Thornwood was unique. Patients performed much of the manual labor on the massive grounds. They performed agricultural duties, as well sewing, and numerous other types of labor. Patients were paid modest wages for their labor, and it was believed that such occupational therapy had a soothing effect and positive impact toward their treatment.

As was the case with most mental health facilities at the time, the mode of patient treatment morphed from the holistic forms of occupational therapy to more physically aggressive and radical forms of treatment that were, at times, brutal. The more aggressive treatments included surgical lobotomies and hydro and electro shock therapy. At one point, doctors at Thornwood placed brain matter of deceased patients in formaldehyde filled jars on full display in some of their buildings. Lola frowned in disbelief as Ruth said, "Believe it or not, they actually thought that it would be therapeutic for the patients to see that." She explained that the horrors of such treatment created the negative stigma attached to many mental hospitals of the time. Over time, a labor shortage was created due to the patients no longer performing the therapeutic occupational labor they once enjoyed. In response, the hospital began to hire laborers and a wide array of other personnel in great numbers, some of whom were permanent but most transient.

"Horrible stories, some true, others mere rumor, began to spread in the mid-1970s about mental facilities like Thornwood Manor," Ruth said. "Several television documentaries depicting the horrors of mental institutions throughout New York State popularized the already growing negative stigma. Shocking footage of horrid conditions with half-naked and malnourished underage patients covered in filth and feces while walking around aimlessly in overly crowded and severely short-staffed facilities shocked the public's conscious and embarrassed state officials. Thornwood was also featured in some of those documentaries."

"We have seen some of these videos on the internet," said Lola. "Do you have any other films here?"

"Unfortunately, we do not," replied Ruth.

Ruth continued to explain the growing and widespread condemnation of the conditions at facilities like Thornwood. This, along with the introduction of modern medicine to treat mental illness, helped put an end to the torturous methods previously used and eventually led to the closure of these types of facilities altogether. In particular, the introduction of medications like Thorazine and other key advancements in medicinal treatment enabled patients to be treated in their homes and other types of medical facilities. This directly led to the sharp decline in the need for mental health hospitals and facilities like Thornwood. "Unfortunately, the system was not equipped to deal with the mass discharge of these patients, and this had a direct impact to the increase of homelessness and prison population in New York State. There are state-wide economic studies performed by analysts detailing this information. I am sure that you will be able to locate these reports if you are interested."

"In 1996, after being in operation for nearly a century, Thornwood Manor closed its doors for good. Today, the grounds of the Village are owned by local developers who hope to modify the property. Years of neglect and vandalism have ravished what is left of the buildings that remain. Nevertheless, many of the buildings still stand today as a testament to a foregone age of mental health treatment." Ruth took a breath, smiled and said, "Well, that's my crash-course on Thornwood Manor." She stood and removed a large box from a shelf behind them containing a limited archival collection on Thornwood Manor. "I'm sorry we don't have more items in our collection," she said. "Most of the medical records were retained by the State, and by the time the facility was closed, there was little appetite to preserve too much of that place."

"Thank you," replied Savoy. "We appreciate the information and the chance to look over anything you may have."

"It's my pleasure," replied Ruth. She looked at both of them and said, "I will leave you to your search. If you need anything, please let me know."

Lola was highly impressed by Ruth's pleasant demeanor and knowledge. She thanked her for providing the brief tutorial.

Savoy and Lola sifted through the documents in the box. They found an old brochure of Thornwood Manor, some medical reports detailing administrative procedures from the 1920s through the 1960s, and some old newspaper articles covering the facility. Savoy was pleasantly surprised to find copies of the original blueprints of Thornwood. "This could help us when we visit this place," he said with a wide grin as he placed them to the side.

Lola retrieved a large stack of scattered pictures from Thornwood. Some were pictures of patients and medical staff strolling the large grounds. "Looks like a peaceful place," said Lola. Other pictures of people dressed in various costumes were among the collection. "I remember reading that they used to put on performances for the patients and staff," said Lola. She removed some group pictures from the collection and shared some of them with Savoy to review. The pictures were each labeled "Staff Picnic" from various years, and large groups of uniformed employees stood smiling in the center of a great lawn.

Ruth entered to room, saw Savoy holding the pictures, and said, "Each year, Thornwood held a large picnic for the entire staff. It was intended to relieve the stress of working in such difficult conditions."

Savoy thumbed through the pictures and spotted one dated April 1977. That was near the time of Adeline's death. On the back of the picture was a list of the names of the employees who were pictured. He then saw similar pictures from random years, each with the same information. Ruth offered to make copies of the pictures for them. Most of the other documents were not informative for their investigation.

Ruth returned with copies of the pictures and they each placed documents back into the box.

Savoy and Lola thanked the woman for her hospitality and left a modest donation for their group before exiting the library.

Committed

It was a rainy Saturday morning. The family's brown Lincoln Continental motored along the Palisades Parkway, tires pulling up rainwater from the puddled roadway. Adeline sat in the rear of the car with the side of her head placed gently against the glass. She counted the trees as they passed while lightly humming to the sweet melody of "Dancing Queen" by ABBA playing through the headphones of her Sony Walkman. She personally identified with the song, particularly the chorus that she had long memorized and identified with about a dancing queen.

The sweet melody soothed Adeline, but it also helped to drown out the sounds of her parents who were quarreling. She wasn't sure if her parents were upset with each other or if they were upset at her. For as long as she could remember, she struggled to understand even the most typical social cues. Obvious or even subtle hints of humor, irony, sarcasm and other emotional signals are often lost upon her. This is one of the many symptoms of Ohr's Syndrome. To make up for that shortcoming, she forever seeks visual confirmation to decipher the emotions of others. This includes staring at people's faces in an attempt to deduce what they are feeling. She had done that this morning, and she saw nothing but anger and pain. To stay out of the fray, Adeline focused on her music…and the trees.

The rain had finally let up as the car exited the parkway. Several winding, tree-lined roads formed an almost mystical portal, invoking wonderful thoughts for Adeline—even though she should have detected an ominous tone. The car turned up a long driveway, and a stone building with barred windows appeared before them. The building was centered among a series of other stone-structure buildings, all set among well-manicured lawns. Across the street was a building with two red garage doors. As one of them opened, Adeline could see a small fire truck inside. She disliked fire trucks because the blaring lights and sirens always hurt her eyes and ears.

Adeline removed her headphones to focus on this new magical and mysterious place. Perhaps they were visiting a friend, or it may be a place for her father to conduct business. Her intrigue was matched by her confusion. In the passenger side rearview mirror, the look on her mother's face seemed to tell a far darker version, something that she should have known to be terrifying. Her father opened his car door, and with a heavy push slammed it shut, shaking the entire car. Her mother continued to glare painfully at the building as her father extracted the wheelchair from the trunk of the car. Adeline opened her door and exited the car to take in the scenery. "What is this place, mommy?" she asked. Her mother could only offer a somber look as her father helped her transport from the car into her wheelchair. Her father grabbed the handles of her mother's wheelchair and said with a stern voice, "Let's go." Adeline looked up toward the sky and, just before they entered the building, she spotted a beautiful cardinal circling in the sky above.

As the trio entered the building, the frigid temperature inside caused Adeline to shudder and grasp her forearms. A strict looking well-manicured man and woman dressed in all white nurses' attire approached them. The man pulled Adeline's father to the side, and her mother conversed with the woman. After a few short exchanges and the signing of documents, none of which Adeline cared to pay any attention to, the woman turned to Adeline and said, "Hello, dear, my name is Mrs. Jones. You can come with me now." Confused, Adeline turned to her mother who struggled to make eye contact before caressing her daughter's hand and said, "It's all right, Addy. You are going to visit with Ms. Jones for a while. Remember, we talked about this. It will be like when you were little and we went to camp. You were afraid then, but you handled it like a big girl. This will be sort of the same thing. Can I count on you to be a big girl?" Adeline nodded her head yes. "Daddy and I will be back later to see you. You'll see."

Adeline scanned the lobby. The white-tiled walls smelled of disinfectant, and despite the presence of several occupants in the hall, there was absolute silence. In her heart, she suspected that she should be afraid, protest, even run, but she could not comprehend why. An older man, similarly dressed in all white, was mopping the floor nearby. He turned to Adeline and she strained to read his facial expressions, but he stoically went about his work. She took another moment to study her surroundings before turning to Mrs. Jones, and with a smile said, "My name is Adeline Marie Deveraux. My friends call me Addy.

You can call me Addy." The woman gave a half smile before narrowing her eyes and said, "That's wonderful, dear. Please follow me," as she turned toward a heavy wooden door at the end of the hall. Adeline smiled and gave her father a hug before turning to her mother. She had been taught that when you hug someone, hug them with two hands, so that your hearts can touch. When she hugged her mother and touched her heart, instead of the warmth she usually felt from her, she could only feel pain. "You be a good girl," her mother whispered.

The woman turned, and as Adeline began to approach, she gestured for her to take off the headphones and said, "Oh, dear, those are not allowed here. Please give them to your mother."

Aghast, Adeline turned to her mother who said, "It will be all right, darling. I will hold onto these for you."

"Mrs. Jones, will they have music playing?"

Mrs. Jones expression was stoic as she said, "Sure. There will be proper music playing. Now, please, let's go. We have a schedule to keep."

As she was being led away, Adeline turned back for a final look at her parents. Choking back tears, her father managed to wave goodbye as her mother openly wept. Adeline wanted to turn and run to them both, but Mrs. Jones, now clutching her upper arm more tightly than before, led her through the door and down a long corridor.

Adeline's mother wept inconsolably as the doctor inched over and said, "Don't worry, Mr. and Mrs. Deveraux. Your daughter will be receiving the finest care at Thornwood Manor."

The Architect

Doug Reynolds always fancied himself an entrepreneur. For as long as he could remember, he'd loved the art of the transaction. At a young age, while most of his friends played sports, Doug attached himself to a toy cash register and fake money where he spent countless hours formulating imaginary business deals. Although they were make-believe, Doug knew that such practices would eventually come in handy as an adult.

Doug was born and raised by a wealthy upper-class family in Dix Hills, New York. He spent most of his childhood focusing exclusively on his schoolwork. He enjoyed playing sports recreationally but preferred to spend most of his evenings at home studying and writing. His interest in academics helped him excel among his peers. Doug received numerous accolades in elementary and middle school which led to honors in high school culminating with a lucrative scholarship at the prestigious Maritime College where he earned degrees in both electrical and mechanical engineering. Later he earned a master's degree in Business Administration. Armed with a well-rounded education, he was ready to rule the business world.

It was the late 1960's and opportunities were beginning to open for Doug. At the same time, the influence of many labor unions grew throughout the country and particularly the New York area. Doug loathed the very concept of a labor union. To him, they were the antithesis to his penchant for individuality and an impediment to his inexhaustible ambition and demand for full control. Mostly, he abhorred unions because they inhibited his ability to maximize profits by manipulating an unskilled non-union workforce.

Everything about his business taught Doug that you earn what you get and those in the way, especially labor unions, are meant to be crushed. Labor unions also possessed negotiating power, which, in his view, stood directly in the path of him and his employees. Thus, Doug made it his life's mission to never engage in a business proposition where he did not have complete authority and power of the operation. As such, Doug would never engage in any business where a labor union was involved.

Long work hours had never allowed much time for romance in Doug's life. After several short-term relationships, he'd married a young aspiring actress from California with a wealthy family. However, his new bride's competing career goals sharply conflicted with Doug's need to be the most important part of her life. As a result, the couple divorced one year later. The bitter divorce had led to huge financial losses for Doug at the hands of his ex-wife and her family's high-powered divorce attorney; losses that had left him scorned for the rest of his life.

Determined to financially recover, Doug continued to accelerate his career goals. His first business venture was a contracting company engaged in lighting installation at large institutions where he partnered with two of his classmates. The business quickly floundered, but not because of a lack of business acumen. Doug surely made up for what his partners lacked. The business ultimately failed because Doug had a different vision from the other two. Doug sought long-term contracts with large institutional universities and medical centers in the New York City area, while the other two wanted to focus the business more on short term and diverse projects throughout the country.

After the dissolution of his first business venture, Doug connected with a group of German engineering investors eager to make a name in the U.S. market. The group manufactured industrial heating and cooling power plants designed to handle the energy demands of large facilities seeking self-sufficiency, and more importantly, cost efficiency. The partnership, named Excel-Haus Enterprises, known in the industry as simply EH, flourished with Doug retaining majority control of the company. In the early 1970s, EH made strong gains in the New York market and eventually became one of the leading power plant designers.

Business was flourishing but, as always, Doug wanted more. It wasn't enough to simply build a plant and move on. His goal was to staff, maintain, operate, and, of course, profit from power plants, and his luck was about the change when in 1972 EH was contacted by representatives of the Thornwood Manor Psychiatric Center who were interested in partnering with them to upgrade its aging power plant. After lengthy negotiations, Thornwood Manor agreed to retain EH to not only redesign the power plant, but to also manage and provide staffing to fully operate the plant for a period of no less than ten years. This was the big break Doug had waited for his entire life. He had full control of a secure, and well-financed, project at a large institution. This was his time, and the sky was the limit.

The Game

Capoeira is an Afro-Brazilian martial art that combines spectacular elements of dance and music. Created nearly 500 years ago by slaves in Brazil, this martial art is as a form of self-liberation. While it seems graceful and fun, and it certainly develops extraordinary reflexes and agility, Capoeira is a potent form of self-defense that consists of circular and straight kicks, takedowns, and spectacular acrobatics. During a routine session, participants form a "roda," or circle, as music is being played from an ancient West African mono-chord instrument and drum, similar to a primitive conga. Together, the music forms hypnotic beats while members enter the middle of the circle to perform various acrobatic moves and sing emotional songs. The spirit and energy of a roda is unmistakable and contagious. Modern day Capoeira classes can now be found in most parts of the world.

After many months and at the persistent urging of Andre "Dre" Carter, his law school buddy turned federal prosecutor extraordinaire, Savoy finally joined a Capoeira class. "Dude" Dre would often say, "I am telling you, Capoeira brings complete health and balance to all who practice it. You must try it. You will be hooked."

Savoy and Dre's professional careers had recently reconnected when Dre assisted him in the investigation of the death of Maria Cruz, Lola's mother. Much has changed in Dre's career in the past year. He now works closely with Richard Ramos who leads a newly revamped cold case crime unit in the Northeast region. Their work in the Maria Cruz case had brought new-found fame for the two men and had also led to whisperings of a career in politics for Dre, but he would never consider such thoughts, *at least not publicly*. Dre prefers to get lost in his work as a prosecutor and adjunct professor in a New York area law school.

On this evening, Savoy and Dre sat in a small bar in the Lower East Side of New York City, still catching their breath from their latest Capoeira session. "So, how's it going? How's Lola and the baby? asked Dre. "I better be the Godfather."

Savoy took a sip of his beer, smiled and said "Good, thanks. Yes, I think you are on the inside track for Godfather," Savoy said with a hint of sarcasm at the foregone conclusion that Dre most certainly would be. Savoy sipped his beer again before continuing, "Dude, I have a new...case."

Dre leaned back in his seat. "Oh, man, I should have known you were up to something. What is it now?"

Savoy explained that Loretta Deveraux had retained him to investigate the death of her 19-year-old daughter. "She had a genetic disorder," he added. "The parents were unable to care for her and had her committed there at 18. A short time later, she was found dead in her room from an apparent suicide."

With a slight grimace, Dre said, "That's rough, man. But if it was a suicide, why are you involved?"

"I know," Savoy replied. "Being dumped in a mental asylum by her parents must have had a profound effect on a young mentally-ill girl. It's conceivable that it was nothing more than a suicide, but her mother insists that she wouldn't have killed herself."

Dre looked sharply at him. "Dude, you have a baby on the way. Isn't there anything better you can do with your time?"

Savoy nodded in agreement. "I know, I know. But you of all people know how it is. There's something with this case that doesn't add up. Anyway, I have a new partner now."

"Who?" Dre asked.

"My better half."

Dre laughed. "Why are you dragging that poor woman around with you on your shenanigans?"

"Are you kidding? She's stronger than both of us. She can handle it. Besides, it will give us the opportunity to spend some time together."

"How romantic," quipped Dre.

Savoy smiled. Dre always had a pragmatic way of viewing the world. "Listen," he said, "I will keep you in the loop if I anything significant turns up." Savoy rubbed his right wrist, sore from tonight's Capoeira session. "Man, I am beat up a bit, but it feels great," he said.

"It's good for you," replied Dre. "You are going to need that agility to keep up with that little one of yours."

They finished their drinks and shook hands before leaving the bar. "Keep me in the loop," said Dre. "Remember what I always say, if you find enough credible physical evidence, I will send in the cavalry."

"Will do," replied Savoy with a smile before saying, "I'll see you next week." Savoy grabbed his bag and left the bar with a sense of relief. The support and resources that Dre had access to always fueled his confidence in these cases. Of course, the information Dre required had to be credible and not circumstantial. Dre would not risk his credibility within the department by embarking on cases that had no chance of resolution, nor would Savoy even ask. They were both keenly aware of the high stakes. Respecting that was an unspoken deal between the two—one never to be tested.

Banished

Bonnie sat nervously in the office of her senior supervisor, Martin Walcott. She was awaiting his critical, overbearing, and unfair judgment of her work. This had, unfortunately, been the norm in her relatively short time at the Rockland County Medical Examiner's Office. The heavy dark leather chair consumed her somewhat tiny frame as she sat gently in it. She glanced around the poorly lit office. Dark wood-tiled paneling, dim lighting, and closed shades supplanted the rays of an otherwise beautiful sunny day. The room had no shortage of symbols aimed at reinforcing Walcott's masculinity and prominence. The walls were adorned with academic diplomas, numerous awards for years of exceptional service in the field of Forensic Pathology, and pictures with prominent industry figures. One autographed photograph enshrined in a dark leather frame has Martin fraternizing with local politicians and business leaders. The wall behind Bonnie's chair had large built-in oak bookshelves stacked with a wide array of medical journals, and above them, protruding from the wall, was the stuffed head of a large black bear, whose lifeless eyes seemed to stare down upon her in a disapproving gaze.

Moments later, Walcott entered the room, closed the door, and sat behind his desk.

Sitting across from him, Bonnie cleared her throat.

He removed a pair of reading glasses from his pocket and placed them on while opening her employment file. He took a moment to review he file before saying, "Do you know why you are here, Ms. Beacham?" He firmly clenched his hands together in front of him on the desk with a serious expression—his eyes beady from the spectacles.

"No, sir, I do not," replied Bonnie softly.

For all the passion she had in her work, Bonnie had as much disdain for Martin Walcott and so many like him. He was a typical figure in the "old boys club," many of whom she'd had the misfortune of meeting, through school and now in her profession. Whatever the field, Bonnie had always been aware of male professionals clamoring for their own acceptance which, once established, formed a group vehemently opposed to outsiders joining their fraternal sanctum. Nary is there a greater threat to these types of men than a smart woman in the same profession. They reveled in any opportunity to shun or otherwise stigmatize a woman from getting "too close." The strategy was usually subtle but nonetheless pervasive. They employ tactics like issuing menial work to their female co-workers or forcing them into the critical eye of over-supervision and strict judgment; all tactics they would never employ against their male co-workers, unless they, too, were, for some reason, forced out of the "clique." Aside from Bonnie, the only other female employee in the office was Shannon Hicks, a young receptionist. Over time, Bonnie and Shannon formed a strong bond; one that was required in this overbearing, misogynistic environment. The two would privately say, "Oorah" to each other— their rallying cry created by Shannon whose younger brother had just enlisted in the Marines.

Walcott leaned back in his chair and then slowly reached into the top drawer of his desk to retrieve a pipe and a small amount of tobacco. He struck a match, drawing upon the pipe until it was properly lit. He took a few drags and released the smoke in her direction. She nearly gagged but refused to give him such satisfaction. After another moment, which felt like an eternity, Martin said, "Ms. Beacham, you have an impressive academic record from renowned schools. But I am fearful that you are not quite making the grade here at this office. Perhaps you should consider a different position, something more… administrative?" Bonnie, now incensed, leaned forward and said, "Can you explain how you have reached that conclusion, sir?"

Martin removed his glasses and placed them softly on the desk. He held a firm gaze toward her for a few seconds and said, "Well, Ms. Beacham, this is a conclusion I have reached based upon my expertise in this field and in running this office. My record speaks for itself and, judging by your tone, it appears that you are challenging my judgment, which is precisely the problem. You seem to have difficulty with authority and following directives from your superiors. Quite frankly, for as zealous as you seem to be in your work, you continuously waste the precious resources of our department."

Bonnie took a deep breath, "With all due respect, I do not know how you—"

"Tell me, Ms. Beacham. How many hours did you incur in the autopsy of Phillip Chin? Or the John Doe brought in last month?" Stunned by his line of questioning, Bonnie attempted to respond, but Martin continued, "And what about the Deveraux girl recently brought in from Thornwood Manor?"

"Sir, my initial inspection of that young woman's body may indicate that—"

"Ms. Beacham, we have been over this again and again. You have been repeatedly advised not to engage in fantasy stories and conspiracy theories. That girl had a severe genetic disorder. She was dumped in a mental health facility by her parents and unable to carry on. As a result, she committed suicide. For God's sake, she was found hanging in her room!"

Seizing on his pause, Bonnie said, "That is one possibility, sir, but there was evidence to suggest other factors. Please hear me out."

"No," he hissed. "We are done here. Or more precisely, *you* are done here, Ms. Beacham. Effective immediately, you are hereby terminated from employment at this office. You will receive pay for your services rendered up to this point and all other compensation owed to you, but as of now you are no longer employed at this office. Do I make myself clear? Oh, and you can rest assured that I will make all efforts to share my assessment of your work record and behavior with all of my colleagues." He then picked up the phone and summoned the security department to have her escorted from the building.

Bonnie sank in her chair. She could not believe what just happened. All her hard work and dreams of serving in this office, all her desires and wishes and, most of all, the promise she had made to her father, had just been crushed in the blink of an eye. She felt tears well up in her eyes, but rather than give him the satisfaction, she rose and extended her hand to shake his.

Stunned by the gesture, he complied, meekly shaking her hand.

Bonnie turned and exited the office as two large security officers appeared at the door. Bonnie made her way to her office to collect her personal items. Shannon looked on from a distance, and when the two made eye contact, Bonnie began to cry. Composing herself before anyone else could notice, she packed her belongings in a box and hastily left her office. Stopping only briefly to offer Shannon a hug and a word of encouragement before leaving the building, never to return.

The Ruins

Nestled in the rolling hills of Rockland County, approximately three miles from the nearest highway, are the remains of Thornwood Manor. Savoy and Lola drove along a road which intersected across the property. From their initial research, they had learned that approximately half of the two-thousand acres formerly used by the facility had been razed to make way for a sprawling golf course. Of the remaining buildings, some were still used by local municipalities for government administrative purposes, but the vast remainder of buildings were abandoned.

On one side of the road, they saw a businessman running into what appeared to be a small courthouse and on the other were several elderly men smoking cigars while riding along in golf carts; both a far cry from what this land was used for long ago. As they passed a bend in the road, two deer spotted their car and quickly scampered into a thick patch of trees. They continued to drive until finally reaching a large patch of land housing the remainder of the abandoned buildings, standing as they once did, only now representing dormant relics of the past.

Savoy parked in a driveway abutting a padlocked fence. A light mist began to fall from the overcast sky as the couple made their way toward the main grounds. They were greeted with an eerie serenity as they walked the same grounds that were once traversed by psychiatric patients and staff, including the young Adeline Marie Deveraux more than 40 years ago. Much to their surprise, the infrastructure of the stone buildings were still in decent shape, albeit covered with ivy and other foliage. Some had broken windows exposing graffiti laced walls inside. Despite the many signs warning of unlawful trespassing, the grounds had attracted many visitors over the years.

Savoy studied a map that he drew from the original blueprints he found at the historical society and quickly located their general location. An ornate cobblestone pathway greeted them near the entrance which led to a large patch of grass surrounded by several buildings, some of which were numbered, and others named. As they neared the doorway of each building, they checked for entry. Most were boarded shut. They spotted a large open window toward the rear of one building, but jagged debris inside thwarted their entry.

They moved along to another large one-story building at the center of the property. The door was unlocked. Inside they could see what was left of an old billiards table, other random sporting equipment, and broken chairs. An abandoned wheelchair with writing scribbled on the back was tucked within a nearby closet. They exited the building and continued their search. According to the map, the young female ward was near the end of the field. It was named the Bradley Building. As they approached the front of the building, Savoy and Lola paused for a moment, realizing that this was the location where Adeline lived and died. They could feel the forces of history pulling on them.

Loretta informed them that Adeline's room was in the rear left corner of the second floor. They walked around toward the rear of the building and could see the window of her room. They continued around the back and saw a large basement window that was open. Savoy pondered the No Trespassing sign and thought about how bad it would be for him, as a lawyer, to be caught trespassing. He kept walking before looking back to see that Lola had already entered through the window and was standing inside the basement. In response to his surprised look, she said with a smile, "Don't worry. If a cop comes, we'll tell him that I'm pregnant and needed a place to use the bathroom." Savoy smiled and shook his head before entering the window behind her.

Similar to the online videos they'd seen posted by urban explorers who filmed their trips through the "ruins" of Thornwood Manor, they saw scattered furniture and other debris strewn about and the walls were covered in graffiti. A random drip of water echoed through the basement and the musty odor was unmistakable. Wielding their flashlights, they made their way slowly up the staircase to the second floor. The deathly silence in the building was momentarily disturbed by a crow cawing in the distance. They turned left and headed to the end of the hall and then to the corner room on the right. A broken door surrounded by shards of glass lay on the floor at the entry to the room. Savoy grabbed Lola's hand and guided her over the broken door and into the room. Other than peaceful emptiness, there was nothing to signify that Adeline had lived and died here over 40 years ago.

Lola explored the graffiti marked room as Savoy neared the corner window. He looked up and noticed three rusted bars near the top of the window. "I think these are the bars that she was found hanging from," he said aloud while grimacing at the thought of how brutal it must have been to have found her like that.

Lola approached from behind, placing her hand on his shoulder as they both stared at the bars. Whether she'd truly died there or not, Adeline's body had definitely been hung there and the imagery was sobering for both of them. Savoy inched toward the window; in the distance, he could see a small bridge spanning over a narrow brook. Lola joined him and said, "Adeline wrote about a creek in one of her letters. She described it as one of the few places that gave her solace. That must be it. Let's go see it."

After snapping numerous pictures of the room, Savoy and Lola exited the building and headed toward the small bridge. It was approximately 75 yards away from Adeline's building. As they neared, they were greeted by another No Trespassing sign hanging from a chain at the foot of the bridge. Savoy paused again, but Lola grabbed his hand and said, "Can't stop now." The crossed over the chain and stood atop the bridge to observe the creek below. "Adeline was right," said Lola. "It is tranquil." On the other side of the bridge, they saw a large smokestack towering over a building.

"That must be the power plant," Savoy said as he studied the map again. "Just like Ruth had said: it was a self-contained city."

They crossed the bridge and visited two small buildings to the left, but both were locked. They then walked to the large power plant building with a facade boasting a series of twenty-foot rectangular glassless windows with some smaller windows near the top. They carefully walked along the front of the building littered with shattered glass. Searching for entry, they strolled along the rear of the building and saw a ramp leading down toward a lower level. Savoy, no longer concerned about the trespassing warnings, led Lola carefully down the ramp littered with debris through a door, hanging loosely from its hinges, and into the former power plant complex.

Strands of light from outside barely penetrated the dark room forcing them to flick on their flashlights. The large rectangular room was lined with cinder block walls and housed large pieces of abandoned machinery and other random equipment. "This reminds me of the power plant at my old job," Savoy mused. They came upon a large wooden oak work bench toward the corner of the room littered with scattered documents and broken parts. Savoy playfully spun the metal lever of a vice situated at the corner of the table. They searched the drawers, and near the bottom, Lola found a set of blueprints. "Check this out," she said. Savoy pointed his flashlight to scan the prints. He then looked up to match the location of the equipment listed on the prints to their location in the room. Approaching four industrial sized vessels of equal size, Savoy pointed to the first two and said, "Those were the air conditioning units. They produced cooling in the summer. Those two on the other side were the boilers used to make hot water for heating in the winter." Pointing at the large pipes, he added, "The system was designed to distribute cold or hot water in underground pipes to each building throughout the entire facility. Quite impressive for its time."

"Easy on the shop talk there," quipped Lola.

He chuckled and replied, "Sorry, I got lost in the moment."

Lola inadvertently kicked some beer cans and other loose debris scattered in the middle of the room, exposing the smooth painted floor.

Savoy smiled and said, "Battleship gray. The same color they use to paint the floors in my old shop."

Lola entered a doorway toward the rear of the plant which led into, what appeared to be, a former locker room. Most of the lockers were knocked to the ground. "Any idea on what we are looking for?" she asked.

"None," Savoy replied. "I don't think there is much left." An adjacent room contained a bathroom with the fixtures still intact. Another room in the rear boasted a broken refrigerator and rusted utensils. "Probably the old lunch room," quipped Savoy. "The stories they must have told here back in the day would have been great. You can't beat that old shop talk." Behind the lunch room, they saw an elongated room with a partially caged door. They each shined their flashlights inside and could see random debris scattered about. They pried open the door and inside lay broken mechanical parts, some large oil drums, a few random fan belts hanging from large hooks protruding from the wall, and large wood-shelved cabinets with rusted nuts and bolts scattered about. "This was probably the supply area for the plant," said Savoy.

They approached several large, gray metal file cabinets within the room. Inside, they found binders filled with random documents, broken tools, and other loose parts. Savoy reached for the bottom drawer of one of the cabinets, opened it slowly, and found a stack of thick ledger books inside. The drawer immediately above that had similar books inside. He removed them and carefully placed them on top of a nearby bench. "Interesting," he said as he blew some dust off the books.

"What have you got?" asked Lola.

"Power plants keep log books to record and communicate important data like operating conditions, which employees were on duty, the repairs that were made, and so forth. I can't believe these are still here."

"When are they dated?" asked Lola.

"It looks like each book contains a year's worth of data chronologically from January to December." They took a few minutes to sort the books in proper chronological order. The books, twenty in all, spanned the years 1972-1982 and were all labeled with "EH" on the cover. This same logo matched the logos found on the machinery and blueprints scattered on the table. "EH must be the name of the company that operated the plant," said Savoy as he jotted the information into his notebook.

Savoy retrieved the book for the calendar year 1977; the year that Adeline died. He flipped through the pages until he found the entries for April 15, 1977: the day of her death. It appeared that four employees worked at the plant that day and they each logged in temperatures of the machinery and random repairs and maintenance they had performed. Lola peered over his shoulder and said, "Her body was found early in the morning, and the time of death was estimated at least a few hours before that, so you may want to check the day before as well."

Savoy snapped his fingers at her sage advice and turned back to the proceeding pages. According to the entries, two employees worked the midnight shift. Their names were Liam Callaghan and Barry Gribbon. Savoy jotted the names down in his notebook. "Wait, my mistake," he said as he continued to read entries more thoroughly. "It appears that Callaghan was out sick that night, and Gribbon ran the whole plant by himself. He signed and initialed at the bottom of his log entries." He removed his cell phone and prepared to take a picture when Lola said, "Just take it. From the looks of things, I don't think that anyone is going to notice it missing." Savoy winked at her and tucked the 1977 log book under his arm.

Savoy shined his flashlight around the room and saw that directly behind some large pumps and motors, there appeared to be a dark, shaft way. They drew nearer, aiming their flashlights into the dark corridor. Four large pipes snaked along the wall of the shaft way, leaving just enough room to walk along the corridor, adjacent to the pipes. At the entrance of the corridor was a cardboard sign hanging from a small chain which read: The Tunnel.

"This is interesting," quipped Lola as she steadied her light down the dark and damp shaft.

As they traveled along the tunnel, they could hear the faint sound of water dripping in the distance.

"Watch out for the rats," Savoy said with a chuckle, much to her chagrin.

They continued along on a slow pace for approximately 50 yards before coming to a wall. To the right was a makeshift two-step wooden staircase leading to what appeared to be a miniature hatch-like door. Savoy stepped up but had to bend low enough to reach the door. He turned the knob and leaned into the door but felt resistance from the other side. He handed Lola his flashlight and the log book so he could push harder with both hands. After a brief struggle, the door eventually pried open. Savoy stepped out and then reached back to help Lola exit as well.

The door slammed shut behind them as they stood to ascertain their location. Much to their surprise, they had traversed the entire length of the plant and ended up only a few yards from the small bridge they had first crossed to get to the plant. Just beyond that they could clearly see the outline of the Bradley Building: the young women's ward where Adeline both lived and died.

Savoy and Lola spent the next hour walking throughout the rest of the property until the rain began to intensify, forcing them to end their search. They ran to the car to escape the rain.

"We are on a roll. Where do you want to go next?" asked Lola.

"The Bronx, to meet Elena Gonzalez," replied Savoy as he looked at her in the 1977 staff picnic picture. "It's time that we meet the person who worked at Thornwood and who was closest to Adeline before she died."

"Let me give her a call," said Lola. "I'll explain who we are and why we are coming."

Requiem

Loretta Deveraux sat in her wheelchair in front of the coffin which held her only child, Adeline. She wore a simple black dress and laced veil. Her eyes were swollen, and her makeup had long been smeared from incessant crying. She held a set of rosary beads interchangeably in both her hands.

She recalled the birth of her daughter. Doctors had feared that the child may suffer complications from her condition, but they could not be sure. Loretta had waved away those notions like one swatted away a flying insect. She knew in her heart that Adeline was destined to be an angel. Although she was on the smallish side at birth, her daughter appeared to grow normally and, despite a delay, her cognitive functioning increased. In fact, the only serious health issue she could first recall was her daughter's non-stop crying at nights. For the first two years of her life, Adeline suffered from extreme baby colic. It was caused by an excessive buildup of calcium in her body—another symptom of Ohr's Syndrome that doctors had not yet discovered at that time.

As Adeline grew, Loretta did her best to assimilate her into school. Her daughter was bright and friendly, but as the learning requirements increased, she began to fall behind. This left her frustrated and dejected. Over time, she was left with only one option. So, some time later, Loretta began to homeschool their daughter and she did all within her power to raise her to be a proper young lady. Lessons in everything from math and science to hygiene and social etiquette were all part of their daily routine. Loretta also strived to accentuate the things that gave Adeline joy. She loved dancing and nature, but most of all, she loved music. Music from all genres and eras played throughout the house every day. Adeline would often hum and sing to the various tunes being played. These were great times indeed for mother and daughter until one fateful day when Loretta suffered a serious fall in their home, leaving her confined to wheelchair for the rest of her life.

Her inability to properly nurture their daughter, coupled with an unruly and close-minded husband, ultimately, led to the decision to have her placed in Thornwood Manor. Now, as she sat before her daughter's coffin, witnessing her lifeless body, Loretta knew that for the rest of her life, the guilt of failing to do more to prevent her daughter from being committed to a mental institution—such a cruel place that became the scene of her death—would forever consume any possibility of joy she could ever have in her life. Gone was her beloved angel and all that awaited her was nothing but sorrow.

With shaky arms, Loretta pressed against the sides of her wheelchair and slowly rose to stand. It had been a while she had done so, but in her mind, nothing would stop her. Some family members rushed over to assist, but she whisked them away. She needed to do this on her own. When she rose, she slowly limped with her disfigured back toward the coffin, clutching her rosary beads tightly. She bent down to kiss her beloved daughter, laid her head onto Adeline's chest, and wept.

Palomita

Elena Margarita Gonzalez lived with her older cousin, Hilda, in a small apartment in a pre-war building in the Bronx. She was born and raised in Santurce, Puerto Rico, and relocated to New York in her early teens. Elena was raised by their aunt, Fortuna, a strong and loving woman who, for years, toiled as a seamstress in a Brooklyn factory, sewing uniforms for American soldiers in World War II. Elena, now in her 70s, has never been married nor had children.

Elena never received a formal education. Her learning was derived from a wealth of life experiences attained from working many jobs of varying types. She had worked as a laborer in a toy factory, a waitress for several restaurants, and had done a great deal of babysitting for her neighbors' children. For many years, Elena also worked in a nearby nursing home, tending to elderly patients. The work was steady but didn't pay well, which always left her searching for more gainful employment.

One evening, Elena saw an advertisement for an orderly position at Thornwood Manor. It was a long commute from her home, but the salary and benefits were far better than any job she hoped to land outside of New York City. She quickly applied and after two interviews, was hired for the position.

In 1965, Elena began her career at Thornwood Manor with high expectations. She knew little of Rockland County, but that did not deter her from hoping to make it a long and productive career. Years of working in a nursing home prepared her to deal with the physical and emotional grind of tending to mental health patients on a daily basis. Elena helped to feed patients, bathe and change them, and soothe them during discomforting times. At other times, she'd have to assist in restraining patients, some suffering from seizures, others who were exhibiting hostile behavior. Whatever was required of her, Elena performed it admirably, responsibly and in a manner which always maintained the dignity of the patients. Throughout the years, she was assigned to varying locations at Thornwood Manor to perform many different tasks. She learned quickly and never complained. One day, Elena was assigned to the young women's ward in the Bradley Building. It was there that she found her niche and spent the rest of her career until retirement.

Elena was respected by the entire staff and beloved by all of her patients. She believed that never having children made her seek out and create strong bonds with the patients she tended to. It was her warm smile and steady hand that put all in her charge at ease. She loved them all and knew them by first name. There were certainly many patients that Elena felt blessed to spend time with, and they adored her, but she had no greater bond than with that of a young woman who came to Thornwood in 1977. A young woman who found great comfort in Elena's warm smile and sweet disposition. That young woman was named Adeline Marie Deveraux. Elena was the person who found Adeline dead in her room and had never gotten over her death. Thus, upon hearing her name from Lola—the stranger who called earlier in the day asking to meet with her—she began to reminisce about the sweet girl who had died in her ward so long ago. The sound of the loud doorbell interrupted her reverie. Using her trusted cane, Elena stood and slowly made her way to the door to greet her guests.

Elena welcomed Savoy and Lola into her apartment. "Hello, please come in. Would you like some coffee?" she asked them. The potent smell of espresso made in the home of an elderly Puerto Rican woman reminded Lola of her youth, and she eagerly replied yes. They sat at a small table inside Elena's kitchen enjoying the coffee and some pastries. Savoy began to ask her about her relationship with Adeline. "I remember the first day she came to Thornwood," said Elena. "She was scared and confused. They usually were when they came there." Elena explained how she took pity on the young girl and made it her mission to look out for her, which eventually led Adeline to gravitate toward Elena. "I saw early on how carefully she studied my face, always looking for comfort. I made it a point to always smile, especially around Adeline." It was easy for them to see how Adeline, a child who struggled to read the emotions of others, would find Elena's warm eyes, broad smile and compassionate demeanor irresistible. "We spent a lot of time walking and talking about nature, music, and life." She continued, "Oh, she loved the music. I called her my "palomita" and treated her like my own.

Lola looked at Savoy to explain that "palomita" was the Spanish word for "little bird." Elena shared with them how Adeline loved birds and would often go for walks on the grounds, counting and even naming them.

As she grew to know her, Elena could see that Adeline had some developmental disabilities, but she always believed that Thornwood was no place for a girl like that. But she wasn't qualified to challenge the diagnosis of a doctor or mental health caretaker, and she was by no means in the position to question the judgment of her parents who sent here there. "All I could do was take care of her as best I could. I loved my little "palomita," said Elena with a look of deep sorrow.

"What was she like?" asked Lola.

"She was sweet," replied Elena. "She spoke softly and always asked a lot of questions. She was also very friendly. Whenever she met someone new, she would always say, "You can call me Addy." This memory brought a brief smile to Elena's face.

"How was she treated there?" asked Savoy. Elena paused and looked at Lola, who quickly sensed the elderly woman's apprehension. Touching her hand, Lola said, "It's ok, Elena. We are here to help. If anybody ever hurt her, we would like to find out."

Elena seemed comforted and said, "There was one person. A man who worked there. He was always standing around making excuses to be at the ward. He always stared at the girls and especially Adeline. One day I saw him in the yard. He was leaning into Adeline who was backed up against a fence. He was touching her waist. I yelled at him to leave her alone and he quickly left. I filed a complaint against him, and I told her parents."

"Do you remember anything about him? Was he a doctor or nurse?" asked Lola.

"No, he always wore a blue work uniform and brown boots. I think he worked in maintenance."

"Do you remember what he looked like? asked Savoy. "No, it was a long time ago."

"What if you saw a picture, would that help?" asked Savoy.

"Maybe...I think so," she replied.

Savoy gestured to Lola who was already retrieving the 1977 staff picture they copied from the historical society. She showed it to Elena who put on her reading glasses. She first smiled in amazement at the picture as she recognized herself seated in front row just three seats from the center. "It was very hard to work there," she said, "but most of us were doing our best for the people," she added.

"Elena," said Savoy, "Do you see the man who was bothering Adeline in this picture?"

Elena scanned the faces slowly. Eventually, she paused at the face of a man standing at the far left in the back row. "This one here, that's him."

Savoy turned the picture over to reveal the names of the employees on the back. He slowly traced his finger until he found the name corresponding with the man pictured. It read: Barry Gribbon, Maintenance Mechanic, Power Plant. He immediately looked at Lola who returned the gaze as they both realized that this is the same individual who was working at the power plant the night before Adeline died. Savoy scribbled some comments in his notebook.

Lola squeezed Savoy's hand to cue him that she would take over the questioning. She then leaned in and gently asked Elena, "What can you tell us about the day you found Adeline?" "¡Ay, Dios mío!" Elena replied sorrowfully while touching her hand to her chest. After a short pause, she said, "It was after 9:00 a.m. and she was not awake yet. Usually, Adeline was one of the first to wake up and walk the halls humming and whistling. I knocked on her door and called out to her, but she did not respond. I started to think that she wasn't there. I opened the door and saw her…" Elena let out a moan and began to weep.

Lola reached out to touch her shoulder and comfort her.

Elena wiped her eyes and composed herself. After a few seconds, she continued, "I saw her hanging by the window. Her eyes were closed. It was horrible." Elena paused again before explaining how her screams immediately alerted the rest of the staff.

Lola cleared her throat and asked, "Elena, everything we have learned about Thornwood suggests that there was overcrowding in those facilities. Why was Adeline alone in a room?" "Yes," Elena replied, "usually there were anywhere between two and four patients in a room. Then the public began to sour against places like Thornwood, many patients began to leave, and there was a great deal of transitioning. Adeline was alone in her room for about two to three months before she died." Elena paused again and said, "My poor palomita."

Savoy felt sympathy for the woman. After all these years, she could still feel the pain of Adeline's death. It really said a great deal about how much she cared for the girl. "Elena," said Savoy, "What do you think happened?"

Elena looked long at each of them before rising to walk toward the kitchen sink. She peered out the window for a moment before looking back at them with a confident glare. "There's no way she would have killed herself."

The passion in her voice caught Savoy and Lola by surprise. She spoke with the same fierce conviction as Loretta.

"Why do you think that?" replied Savoy. Elena returned to sit at the table between them. She raised her index finger firmly and said, "Because she was a gentle girl. Yes, she was sad about being away from home, and yes, she sometimes felt that she was not worthy, but Adeline had a disability. She never really understood the type of place Thornwood was or why she was there. And her sense of time was different than most. To her, it was like she was just visiting and any day her parents would come for her. You ask me why I don't believe that she would have killed herself: It's because she had hope and she never lost it."

Savoy nodded and paused a moment longer, acknowledging the strength in her words. "You've been very helpful, Elena. Is there anything else you can tell us?"

Elena paused for a moment and then stood and walked slowly toward a cabinet in the kitchen. She removed a small wooden box and raised the lid from the top. After shuffling some of the papers inside, she removed a photograph and placed it carefully on the table in front of them. Savoy slid it over and saw a strange image of two deer stag heads with interlocking antlers and a cross shape drawn on the inside of each eye.

"What's this?" asked Lola.

Elena sat down, pulled in her chair and cleared her throat before saying, "The morning that Adeline was found dead, I saw a card on the floor. It was a business card that I had never seen before. I picked it up and looked at it, and, without thinking, I put it in my pocket. Then the police came, and some doctors came to look at her body. They asked us to leave the room. For the rest of the day, I did my best to carry on with my duties, but it was so very hard. That night, I cried so much that I couldn't sleep. I sat up and remembered that I still had the card and took it out of my pocket to look it over. It frightened me. I thought, where could it have come from? What did it mean? So, I took out my camera and snapped a picture of it, and the next day I returned the card to my supervisor. I saved the picture, along with some of the other items I had from the hospital. I never found out what it means, but I knew that it was bad. I could feel it in my heart and I still do."

Savoy used his cell phone to take a picture of it before returning it to Elena.

For the next hour, Elena continued telling them all that she could recall about Adeline's life and her sad death, along with her work at Thornwood Manor.

As they prepared to leave, Elena said, "Please let me know if you find anything." And she offered them each a brief hug before they left.

Graveyard Shift

Barry Gribbon entered the parking lot of the Thornwood Manor Psychiatric Center excited about his job interview. Black Sabbath's "Snowblind" was blaring on his radio and the heat was set on high in his 1970 gold Plymouth Duster. He paid only a few hundred dollars for the car—a steal after duping a local junkie. It was November 16, 1975; a date he'll always remember because it was also his late father's birthday. It would be nice, he thought, if he could finally land the career job his father never thought he could get. Barry was told to enter toward the rear of the power plant building, where a trailer was temporarily stationed as the makeshift office of plant manager, Doug Reynolds.

At precisely 1:10 p.m., Barry knocked on the trailer door and a female voice yelled for him to enter. He was 10 minutes late for his scheduled meeting time. He failed to properly secure the door behind him, and a cold breeze knocked some loose papers off the desk of a woman sitting near the entrance, prompting an immediate look of disgust from her. Barry secured the door and apologized while sizing up the woman. She was a buxom brunette, wearing knee-high brown boots, tight jeans, and an even tighter sweater accentuating her large breasts. Unfazed by his presence, the woman asked Barry to have a seat before reapplying her lipstick.

A few moments later, Doug entered the trailer. He was wearing a heavy wool coat and a white construction helmet. Barry stood to greet him, and the two entered a separate office near the rear of the trailer. "Angela," Doug yelled as he sat at his desk, "Can you fix me a cup of coffee, please?" Barry took a seat by Doug's desk, which was strewn with large blueprints, several thick binders filled with documents, and some loose tools.

Doug opened a cabinet draw and removed a folder filled with resumes. "Barry Gribbon, right?" he asked.

Barry nodded affirmatively.

Doug removed Barry's resume from the file and quickly reviewed his work history. He then asked Barry some random questions about his experience, which clearly seemed more rhetorical than substantive. Doug then said, "The hourly pay is the industry standard and the job is non-union. The plant operates year-round, 24 hours a day, broken up into three 8-hour shifts. The only open positions we have now are on the midnight shift. Do you have a problem with that?"

"No. I would much rather work the midnight shift anyway," replied Barry. "Where I used to work, we called it the Graveyard shift."

Doug looked over his resume one more time and said, "Great.

You're hired. You can start next week."

The two rose to shake hands as Angela entered the office to bring Doug his coffee. Both men stared at her ass as she exited. "We look forward to having you here at Thornwood Manor," said Doug.

Barry thanked him and left the trailer. And that was it. In approximately ten minutes, less time than it took for Doug's secretary to prepare a cup of coffee, Barry Gribbon was hired to be a maintenance mechanic at the new power plant at Thornwood Manor—even though his new employer had failed to discover that he had limited experience and a criminal record, which, of course, was concealed by a highly-exaggerated and falsified resume. Barry exited the trailer and entered his car. Beaming with pride, he took a deep breath before slapping his hand on the dashboard and triumphantly said, "Eat shit, Dad!" He then started his car and sped away.

Dancing Queen

It was a cold December day just after Christmas. Precipitation from the evening before had left the area magnificently blanketed in fresh snow, making the grounds of Thornwood Manor seem more like an Ivy League college than a psychiatric facility. Elena surprised Adeline with some fresh homemade cupcakes with strawberry frosting: her favorite. They had been planning this personal party for some time now. Just a few days prior, Adeline's parents came for an all-too-brief visit, which left the girl saddened, so Elena had made it her mission to cheer her up. As they snacked on the cupcakes, Elena said, "I have a surprise for you!" Adeline's eyes widened with anticipation as Elena removed a small box from her bag. Adeline tore through the wrapping to find a Sony Walkman. "It is second-hand from a thrift shop," Elena said, "but it works just fine." Adeline leaped into Elena's arms to hug and thank her. Elena then removed a cassette tape from her pocket and held it up. "It has your favorites," she said, "including Dancing Queen." Adeline studied her gift excitedly. She had not had her own personal source of music since being committed to Thornwood. She then leaned into Elena to thank her again, squeezing her arms tightly around the woman. Elena let out a chuckle before saying, "Now, remember, don't play it too loud. We don't want them to take it away from you."

Adeline placed the cassette tape into the device and played the music. She rose to the rhythmic beat of "Dancing Queen" and began to dance with joy.

Elena watched with content as Adeline twirled gleefully to the music, seemingly without a care in the world. While she felt a true measure of satisfaction at offering this gift to Adeline, Elena could not help but pity the poor girl. Yes, she had some difficulties with her condition, but she felt that this was no place for her. She needed a home, her parents, and a life. She needed to dance and be one with her music, to experience art and poetry, to smell flowers and run in a field. She needed to live a "normal" life, but her confinement to this wretched place deprived her of all of that. Here she was, like a delicate bird, trapped in a cage, unable to spread her wings.

Adeline reached out to Elena, urging her to rise, and the two joined hands in joyous dance. Elena wore a brilliant smile on her face for she knew that Adeline was forever watching her facial cues, but deep down she also knew that this poor soul needed her, and she would not let her down. Having never had children of her own had forever left her feeling incomplete; Elena swore, from that day forward, to look out for Adeline as if she were her own child.

Do What Thou Wilt

Lola spent hours on the internet searching for any information that could shed light on the strange image that Elena had shared with them. She eventually located a bookstore in White Plains, New York that deals in rare books and symbology. She called and made an appointment with Jonah Stern, a young clerk at the store, who was a so-called "expert" on such topics.

Unsure of what to expect, Savoy and Lola entered the musty shop located on a dark block. A large bell fixed to the door rang announcing their entrance. They were greeted to the background ambiance of Gregorian chants and the pungent smell of amber incense. A young lady was exiting the store as the couple entered. Her nose and eyebrows were pierced with studded jewelry. Savoy held the door open for the woman who peered at him before quickly exiting the store. There appeared to be no other patrons inside. As they approached the counter, a man greeted them with a half-smile. He was seated on a stool at the front counter reading a leather-bound copy of "Purgatorio" by Dante Allighieri.

"Hello," Savoy said. "We're looking for Jonah Stern."

"I'm your guy," Jonah replied without looking up. What can I do you for?" Before they could respond, he raised his eyes, scanned them for a moment, and quickly apologized for his curt reply. He carefully placed the delicately bound book on the counter behind him and said, "Sorry guys. We usually get some real…eccentric…characters in here. It helps to keep up a serious persona. How can I help you?" He was not at all what they expected. He was a relatively young man with long hair tied back in a ponytail, a full beard, and piercing blue eyes. Each of his fingers were tattooed and he had a pentagram shaped charm hanging on a chain from his neck.

"We heard that you probably know more about secret societies than anyone, so we're hoping that you can give us some input," said Savoy.

"Secret societies," replied Jonah with a chuckle. "Is that what the lay people call it these days? Anyway, thank you for the compliment." Jonah spread his arms and gestured toward the reading section of the store, mostly shelves stacked with books and a large, worn, black-leather armchair. "As you can see, I spend a lot of time researching a variety of things. But, yeah, so-called "secret societies" have existed among us for centuries," he said. "In the eighteenth century, the Freemasons were founded in England. They came from the Stonemasons who built the cathedrals in the middle ages. Today, they are estimated at nearly four million members. Hellfire Clubs were also formed in England and Ireland at this time under the doctrine of Sir Francis Dashwood.

The group was made up of the social elite and was rumored to have engaged in black magic and sexual debauchery." Jonah went on to explain that in the late 1800s, the English occultist, Aleister Crowley, founded Thelema, a practice with the mantra, "Do what thou wilt shall be the whole of the law." This, he reasoned, was sort of a weird mix of Tantric Yoga and Black or Sex Magic, where members wore masks and partook in elaborate rituals and alleged satanic worship.

"Of course, you've heard of the Illuminati and the New World Order," he continued. "With their "All Seeing Eye," their membership is alleged to include high profile celebrities and politicians who manipulate modern currency and operate in pretty much every corner of our society. Today, there are all kinds of groups, and with them comes a growing level of suspicion by people who others like to call "Conspiracy Theorists." Some believe, as do I, that planes fly nefariously in our skies releasing chemicals or "chemtrails" comprised of chemical and biological agents into the atmosphere. The belief is that they do this to control the weather and the population. There are others who believe that 9/11 was an inside job: just another false flag for the U.S. to plunge us into an endless war couched as a fight for democracy when it was nothing more than a ploy to seize oil and other natural resources from other countries. You also have the Flat Earthers..." Jonah paused to catch himself before saying, "Anyway, I digress."

Savoy, a lifelong skeptic of such topics, remained unimpressed. He was a product of an education in law coupled with life experience. In his youth, Savoy generally scoffed at such notions. He could, at one point, accept the possibility of the existence of a creature like Bigfoot, but overall, he was not a believer of such things. He cleared his throat and asked, "Jonah, you seem like a real smart guy. Do you really believe all of this stuff?" "Some of it, yes, some I'm not so sure," replied Jonah.

"But I tell you what, I definitely believe in a person's right to question anything and everything. After all, that is what keeps governments and society in check." Reading Savoy's continued skepticism, Jonah asked, "What do you do for a living, Mr. Graves?" After replying, Jonah followed, "A lawyer deals with a case, he or she follows a set of allegations, applies the relevant law, and then draws a conclusion. Same thing here. I follow a set of allegations, apply the relevant data, and draw a conclusion. Is there really much of a difference?"

Savoy studied the young man. He seemed wise beyond his age, which Savoy estimated to be no more than his mid-twenties. He also seemed to possess a solid conviction and a strong desire to research many things. In many ways, Jonah reminded Savoy of himself. While Savoy practiced law and investigate cold cases, Jonah served as a guardian of knowledge, covering everything from modern topics to those of antiquity. He immediately took a liking to Jonah. "I'm sorry if I seem a bit skeptical," said Savoy.

"No worries," replied Jonah. "I get that all the time. Now, how can I help you?"

Savoy and Lola explained that they were looking into the mysterious death of a young woman at Thornwood Manor in 1977.

His eyes grew wide and he said, "My father told me all kinds of stories about that place when I was growing up."

Savoy and Lola explained their mission to him and told him that a suspicious card was found in Adeline's room the day her body was discovered. Savoy removed a copy of the image that Elena saw on the card and showed it to Jonah. He studied the two large stag heads with small interlocking antlers and cross shapes in the eyes of each stag for a few moments before saying, "Hmmm. This is interesting."

"What is the significance of that?" Savoy asked.

Lost in thought, Jonah ignored the question and reached for a nearby leather bound book filled with ancient symbols and writings. Savoy looked at Lola with a slight grin. They were each impressed by Jonah's desire to help.

He pointed at a symbol in the book and laid it on the table. "You see this? The two headed eagle with a crown? That is a prominent symbol of the Freemasons. These groups like duel-headed figures. To them it expresses the duality of mankind: one representing purity and innocence and the other representing sin and vulgarity." He scanned further throughout the book but was unable to find anything that resembled double headed stags.

Jonah stood and quickly walked toward the front door, closed the shade, and locked it. "Give me a minute to look through my secret stash," he said with a slight grin. He went to the back of the store and returned with a larger leather-bound book. The book was aged, but not dusty. He carefully placed the book on the counter and put on white leather gloves before feverishly turning the pages. He then stopped on one page and scrolled down toward the bottom. "There," he said. "I knew that image looked familiar. That's from the Order of the Tempest." He looked at the image again and matched it to the symbol he had in his book. He then looked at Lola and Savoy and said, "Tempest is a sect of a group that was originally formed in London in the latter part of the Nineteenth Century. The group was known for the infamous Venetian Bauta masks they wore during ceremonies."

"Ceremonies?" replied Lola.

"Yes, perverse sexual, and sometimes violent, events. They wore the masks in a twist to hide their elitist status and salacious activities. That whole duality of man belief. Anyway, in the early Twentieth Century, a part of the group immigrated to the United States and settled in the outskirts of major cities such as New York, Boston, Providence, and New Haven. Over the years, the group is alleged to have grown to include very powerful members of their societies and professions, including prominent members of the medical, judicial, business, and entertainment industries. This group thrives on secrecy, so only members of this group would have a card like this." As he studied Elena's photograph again, Jonah pulled out his cell phone and asked if they would mind if he took a picture so that he could study it further. They were happy to oblige.

Jonah went on to explain that a group like Tempest morphed from being a pseudo-religious organization, although several members of the clergy and local politicians are rumored to be part of the group, into a fraternal order that has adopted the collective belief that, given their extreme wealth and social status, they are free to act above the law entirely for their pecuniary gain. Corrupt industrial, business, banking and real estate practices, along with gambling, prostitution, and even sex-trafficking were all within their alleged acts. Theirs is a dogma which suggests that the law, and all other societal norms, are beneath the reach and scope of their power. "Members of a group like this are free to act out on their fetishes without impunity," said Jonah. "Their debauchery is above reprisal. If one were to face legal implications, another would usurp his authority to ensure that such problems would disappear. Judges, lawyers, and other law enforcement officials are all on the payroll. So, too, are politicians for their lobbying aspirations, athletes for their various gambling rings, and sex workers. If it is sinful, unlawful, and most of all, lucrative, this sophisticated mafia of professionals are sure to be involved."

Jonah paused to study Savoy and Lola. It was clear to him that they failed to fully understand that gravity of his words. "How can

I explain it to you in a way you'd better understand?" He paced for a bit, then snapped his fingers. "Ah," he said, "Did you ever see Stanley Kubrick's movie *Eyes Wide Shut*?" They both nodded yes, and he continued, "There are never-ending themes of the hidden symbolism in that movie in relation to modern day secret societies. Clues that the untrained eye would easily miss. You know, symbols hidden in plain sight. For instance, remember that scene where Tom Cruise and Nicole Kidman entered a party of a friend and they get separated in the home and they were tempted to cheat on each other?" Without waiting for their answer, he continued. "Well, if you have a sharp eye like mine, you will notice that inside the house there was the star of Ishtar, the Babylonian goddess of fertility, love, and sexuality. Her worshippers engaged in wild orgies all in her name. Themes of temptation and sex are obviously portrayed throughout the movie."

Savoy and Lola were captivated as he continued. "Then there were the obvious dangers like the fact that there were very powerful people who belonged to a group like that." Jonah narrowed his eyes and said, "These are the kinds of groups that are lurking out there today. The group depicted in that movie was a group like Tempest. I must warn you both. A group like this has countless people on the payroll, and they could all be ruthless. You're probably being watched right now. I would be very careful if I were you. You don't want to fuck with these people." At that moment the telephone rang, startling all of them. After a brief pause, Jonah answered the call as Savoy and Lola rose from their stools. "Thank you, Jonah," Savoy said. "This has been a tremendous help. If you find out anything, please do not hesitate to call me." Savoy handed him his business card and they shook hands before leaving.

As they exited the store, Savoy scanned the street for any suspicious looking vehicles before quickly entering the car and locking the door. He looked nervously at Lola.

"Don't say it," she said.

"Look," said Savoy, "You heard his warning. The last thing I want is to put you and the baby in any danger."

"I told you that I am in this for the long haul," said Lola, slightly arching her achy back.

"And you will be," replied Savoy. "You can continue with research from home. Besides, we have made some good progress already."

Lola would not be deterred. She had committed to assisting in this case, and other than some quirky advice from an eccentric clerk in a bookstore about a mysterious group that may or may not exist, there was nothing to suggest that they were in any kind of danger. "I tell you what," she said, "Let's continue for a bit longer and if anything, actually threatening, happens then I will head back to work from home. Sound good?"

He nodded and leaned over to kiss her on the cheek before driving away from the dark street.

Displaced

It was another busy day at the Rockland County Medical Examiner's Office and Martin Walcott was struggling to keep up with his schedule. Two new bodies entered the office: Charles and Helen Wellington, a husband and wife who died in a terrible crash on the Saw Mill Parkway. There was also the John Doe, a young male found dead from an overdose in a home in Pomona. And just last week, the body of Adeline Marie Deveraux, an apparent suicide, came in.

He sipped on his coffee as he planned the assignments of his staff. He appointed David Chen, his senior examiner on the Wellington case. Charles Wellington was a renowned surgeon in the area, and he wanted his most experienced examiner on the case to ensure the best possible handling. He then appointed Damon Schiff to the John Doe case.

Schiff had been overworked as of late, and giving him a John Doe case, without the demands of a speedy result, seemed appropriate. He had previously assigned Bonnie Beacham to handle the Deveraux case. Since it was a suicide from Thornwood Manor, he felt comfortable giving her that case. Of course, he would be sure to oversee her work. He couldn't leave anything to chance.

He finished up some paperwork and planned to leave for the day when the telephone rang. He reluctantly picked up the receiver.

"Mr. Walcott?" said a male voice on the other end of the receiver.

Walcott immediately recognized the voice. A chill ran down his spine. "Yes, sir," he replied.

"We have a situation," said the man. "The body of a young woman was recently brought into your office. A young female named Adeline Marie Deveraux from Thornwood Manor."

"Yes," replied Walcott. "Her body came in last week." He then paused, allowing the man to continue.

"Mr. Walcott, it is very important that you understand clearly what I'm about to tell you. It is of utmost importance that the cause of death in the Deveraux case be ruled a suicide."

Martin responded, "Yes, I believe that it what was—"

"Mr. Walcott. Under no circumstances shall her death be considered anything other than a suicide. We do not need any negative press from this. Do I make myself clear?"

Walcott stared at the diplomas on his wall. He pretended for a moment that he was a man of integrity and conviction. But deep down he knew that any shred of those qualities, if they ever existed, had long since been erased. He was keenly aware that he sold his soul long ago in exchange for money and security in pursuit of a lasting professional legacy. He was also aware that in order to get all of those things he had to pledge his loyalty to a dark force, whose orders must be obeyed without question. Walcott jotted down some more information before stating, "Yes, sir. I understand. Thank you, sir."

Walcott hung up the phone and sprinted out of his office toward examination room #3. It was the smallest of rooms that always went to the most inexperienced examiners. In this case it was issued to Bonnie. He immediately entered and saw Bonnie wearing surgical gloves, a mask, and goggles, standing over Adeline's body which laid on the steel examination table. Bonnie raised her head upon his entry. "Ms. Beacham," he said. "There has been a change of plans. I need you to take over the John Doe case. Damon will be handling this case going forward. Please give me a complete report of your findings on this matter."

Bonnie was puzzled. She had already begun extensive work on the body and had even begun to formulate her own impressions about the cause of death. She privately suspected that foul play may exist, but she kept those beliefs to herself, at least until the results of the testing she had ordered came back. She had already made that mistake once and had been ridiculed and called a conspiracy theorist. She would not make the same mistake again. Ultimately, she knew not to question his authority. Whether it was politics or misogyny or just the fact that she was still relatively new and wanted to make a name for herself, she knew that resistance was futile. Bonnie lowered the mask to her neck and replied, "Yes sir." She cleaned up and gave one last look at Adeline's body before shutting the lights and exiting the room.

All Access

It was a warm spring day and Barry was working overtime on the front end of a double shift. Nicknamed the "hyena" by his coworkers, Barry never passed up a chance to gobble up overtime whenever it was available. Most of the other employees had families they were eager to return to after work, but Barry lived a solitary life, so he welcomed the reprieve from his loneliness by being busy at work.

After lunch, Barry left the power plant and walked the grounds. The opportunity to escape the noisy machinery, hot climate, and monotonous repetition of the plant was something he relished. He made a slow, steady walk to the maintenance supply shop: a small building, not far from the plant. Known as the "Cage," this building housed a myriad of supplies, tools, and other random equipment

103

necessary for all of the trade work performed at the facility. The Cage is under the direction of Winston Charles, a tall thin man known for his hearty laugh, good-natured demeanor, and a heavy Jamaican accent. For more than 20 years, Winston had been the fierce guardian of the supplies in the Cage. Prior to his tenure, the facility was plagued with poor inventory control and a rash of thefts. Thus, he would never tolerate employees meandering throughout the Cage unaccompanied, lest they stuff their pockets with loose inventory.

Barry entered the Cage and greeted Winston. It had been some time since he'd seen the man because of their different work schedules. Winston was preoccupied with a soap opera playing on a small television adjacent to the front counter. Typically, and in a feeble attempt to conceal it from management, Winston would cover the television with a perfectly trimmed cardboard box that fit over the device. It was the worst kept secret but one that management never truly objected to, unless work wasn't being completed.

After engaging in small talk, Barry asked Winston if anyone was in "the spot." A soft leather reclining chair neatly tucked behind a large rack of equipment out of public view. It was indeed a prime location for workers seeking to get some rest during working hours, without management knowing about it. Thus, "the spot" was in high demand and strictly on a first come first serve basis. Winston never objected to any of the workers claiming the seat so long as they remained within his eyesight. Luckily, for Barry, it was available, and he was granted access.

Moments later, Steve and Robert, both employees from the power plant entered the Cage. They were transporting a large barrel of motor oil with a hand truck. Hearing the two men enter, Barry peeked out from behind his perch and said, "What's up, boys?" This was his feeble method of announcing that he had claimed the prized nook. Steve nodded and Robert replied sarcastically, "What's up, numb nuts? Working hard again, huh?" Barry detested Robert. Not only did he resent the man for constantly flaunting his seniority and experience over Barry, but also because ever since he began working at Thornwood, Robert never passed up an opportunity to ridicule Barry for his solitary lifestyle and brutish looks. "Hey, Barry" said Robert, "Get any ass lately?" as he elbowed Steve, seeking reinforcement. "Probably not," he continued. "You couldn't get laid in a whore house with a fistful of fifties."

"Fuck off," said Barry as he reclined in his seat.

The three men spoke for a few minutes and Robert asked Winston where they should store the barrel of oil they had brought. "Is it empty?" asked Winston. "Just about," they replied. Winston reached above the counter for a set of keys to a room adjacent to the Cage where the drums of oil were kept. He peered over at Barry who appeared to be taking a nap and then stepped out from behind the counter to escort the two men next door to deposit the barrel.

Once the three men were outside, Barry opened his eyes. He was not sleeping at all. In fact, he was waiting for this opportunity and was determined to capitalize on it. He rushed toward a steel cabinet under the counter. This is where copies of the master keys to the entire Thornwood Manor facility were kept. He quickly slipped off one of the keys from the ring and tucked it into his pocket. The men were returning, and Barry did not have time to return to the spot.

Winston spotted him and said, "What are you doing?"

Fumbling to produce a clever answer, Barry said, "Nothing. I'm just heading back to the plant."

"Sneaky prick," said Robert as Winston glared at Barry as he made a slow pace toward the door doing his best to act naturally. He glanced back at the three men and said, "Later boys." Barry exited the building quite pleased at the cunning way he'd handled the situation. More importantly, he now possessed a copy of the master key for every door at the facility and grew excited at the prize such unfettered access would grant him.

Visitation

Thomas Deveraux stood outside of the patient common hall at Thornwood Manor. Fraught with anxiety, he lit a cigarette and leaned against the stone wall. Of course, he was always eager to see her, and he felt that this was the best place to ensure her safety but visiting his daughter in this place always made him uneasy.

Growing up in Rockland County, everyone knew about Thornwood Manor. Over time, and fueled by ignorance of mental health, a negative stigma had formed about the facility. Children like Thomas were raised to believe that it was the place that housed the "crazies," a place for the uncontrollably misguided souls forever burdened by mental illness. The stigma was so prevalent that Thomas felt uneasy in even calling the facility to seek assistance for his daughter. He eventually mustered enough courage to call, and after several meetings, he made the decision to have Adeline committed there. It was all he could think of doing. With his long work hours and his wife Loretta, plagued with a debilitating back injury that prevented her from adequately caring for their daughter, his options were limited. Thus, having Adeline committed for her protection was, in his mind, the only option, and no one would be able to convince him otherwise.

He drew a deep drag from his cigarette and watched as several patients, all with varying forms of mental illness, passed through the hall. Some were alone, others required assistance. After a few minutes, he returned inside the hall where Adeline was seated at a table chatting with her mother. She was gushing with anticipation over the upcoming holiday show—a long-held tradition at Thornwood. Adeline had been rehearsing for months, and, although she was to perform a relatively small part, the pride with which she spoke made her eyes sparkle. Adeline also spoke glowingly about her friendship with Elena, Rosemary, and some of the other friends she had made while there.

A commotion ensued, disrupting their discussion, as a patient erupted in a sudden and violent seizure. Thomas quickly stood, unsure if he should assist, as Adeline placed her fingers into her ears to drown out the screams. Several agonizing minutes passed until two medical staff employees rushed in to stabilize the patient. Loretta looked at her jittery husband. An encounter like this only perpetuated his nerves and she knew that he would soon be eager to leave. Adeline also studied his face searching for clues, but she was unable to decipher his feelings.

"Adeline," said Loretta, recapturing her daughter's attention. "We are very excited about the upcoming show. Keep practicing. You will be great." Pleased with her parents' interest and enthusiasm for the show, Adeline smiled widely. After a few uneasy minutes, the family exited the hall for a short walk before their departure. Thomas gently pushed Loretta along in her wheelchair as Adeline skipped ahead in high spirits. After all, her parents were with her, it was a beautiful day, and she had a part in the upcoming holiday show. They neared the front entrance, and, after a short embrace with each of her parents, they left their daughter who skipped away humming to her favorite songs.

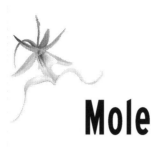

Mole

Stuart Hennessy came from a family with a long history in law enforcement. His father was a highly decorated detective at a renowned precinct in the lower east side of New York City. His uncle also served as detective in the Bronx. Both his father and uncle were inspired to join law enforcement by Stuart's grandfather, Patrick Hennessy, who was a hard-nosed beat cop in the Gramercy Park area of New York. Growing up, Stuart always heard the tales of tough crime fighting. With such a history, there was little doubt that he would also join law enforcement.

Stuart, nicknamed "Stu," graduated from the police academy in 1982. He began his career at a precinct in Harlem. Years on the beat taught him to be a tough and smart cop. He later became a detective just like his father and uncle. But to Stu, there was something "stale" about being a detective. Craving more, he applied to be an agent with the Federal Bureau of Investigations, a decision that drew great consternation from his family. "I can't believe that you want to be a fucking fed," his grandfather had said a few months before he died. His father and uncle were equally disapproving of his career choice. The idea of him joining the government instead of performing local police work was revolting to them. Some years later, Stu's father and uncle retired and passed away. They had never gotten over his decision to join the FBI.

Stu had served as an FBI agent for 28 years. He had always been a proud and reliable agent, but in his later years, and with no real opportunities for growth for a man of his age, Stu grew frustrated at never being able to get ahead. This had left him jaded and, over time, led Stu to undertake practices that would run afoul of agency protocol and eventually the law. That, of course, is how he would describe it, but in reality, Stu was dirty and had been for many years. To him, the occasional lifting of cash from a dirtbag dealer during a narcotic bust was a harmless offense. He had even gone so far as to plant evidence on a suspect to ensure a successful conviction in a case. Yet, these unlawful practices were few and far between and never fully paid the bills of a man struggling to afford living in his hum-drum two-bedroom home in Ozone Park.

Naturally, Stu's activities remained unknown to law enforcement. To them, he was a seasoned veteran of the force. Sure, he was crude and far from the professional grade of his newer, younger, and more educated colleagues, but no one would ever suspect that Stu would defile his badge and betray the agency. Unfortunately, for Stu, there were others who had set their sights onto him. Thus, it did not take long for Stu to become prone to blackmail and extortion by Tempest: a group who, once they'd set their hooks, would never let go. In exchange for not exposing his criminal activities, and a small monthly stipend, Stu was required to provide information, and lots of it, to the group.

Over the years, Stu had acted as an informant for Tempest. His simple, yet incredibly risky task was to report the status of any investigation that included Tempest members. Stu was never truly comfortable with this arrangement, but he quickly came to realize that the group's reach was vast. He was keenly aware of their influence, both above and below his pay grade. Stu once attempted to cease his services with the group, but when that was met with threats of criminal exposure, and even death to him and his family, he reluctantly agreed to carry on with his services.

Over time, Stu began to justify his work with Tempest. It wasn't all bad, he thought, and the money was commensurate with the task demanded of him. They needed an inside man, a mole on the force who provided unfettered access to important information from the unsuspecting presence of a grizzled veteran. Stu was their man. It was not as if he had much of a choice anyway.

Months earlier, Stu applied for a transfer to the northeast FBI cold case task force in Rye, New York. A specialized unit led by commanding officer, Richard Ramos, who rose through the ranks for his success rate on cold cases. With advancements over the years in DNA mapping and other technology valuable in crime solving, it had become imperative for the FBI to greatly enhance the lab of this department. The optics of solving decades old cases was politically expedient and sent a strong public message that the agency never gives up on its quest for justice. After a great deal of lobbying by Ramos and other leading figures, the agency agreed to pour an influx of funding to procure vast new resources for his task force. This included hiring more agents and acquiring the newest technology to help solve crimes that had occurred long ago. Armed with a state-of-the-art lab, Ramos' team of forensic scientists, affectionately known as the "Bloodhounds," were now supplemented by a technological team that specialized in computer and electronic equipment and other modern advancements. Of course, the department still required manpower to perform solid investigative work, and after several interviews and a background check into his work, Stu was awarded a position in the department.

On the day Stu reported to headquarters in Rye, he entered the building wearing a faded brown suit. His tie was too short, and his shirt needed to be tucked in, but he had no time to worry about his disheveled appearance. He had an appointment and could not be late. After a brief wait, Stu was greeted by Agent Haverstraw who escorted him to Ramos' office. Ramos, who has having a meeting, rose to greet Stu. The two shook hands and Ramos said, "Stuart, welcome aboard. I'm glad you're here. We are going over some details on a new case. There is someone I would like to introduce you to." He turned to greet the man, who was now rising from his seat. "Stuart," said Ramos, "Meet Andre Carter."

High Demand

After completing his contract at Thornwood Manor, Doug Reynolds moved on and had seen a great amount of success over the years. He oversaw the design, construction, and management of many power plants in hospitals, universities, and other businesses throughout New York. He had been featured in numerous magazines covering the engineering industry. Indeed, Doug had never doubted his abilities or business acumen. He was well educated and possessed the necessary skills, grit, and hustle to succeed in his profession. And according to his professional profile on LinkedIn, Doug currently oversaw the operation of a large meat processing plant in Jamaica, New York.

Savoy and Lola had contacted him earlier that day, and although

Doug could not commit to a specific time to meet, he did suggest that they pass by in the early afternoon. They parked across the street from the busy plant, hoping to catch him. They entered through a large doorway and were met by a set of wide vinyl strip curtains hanging down to the floor to preserve the temperature inside of the plant. Savoy peeled back some of the coverings allowing them to enter. They were immediately met with the stench of raw meat from hanging slabs and the loud sounds of cutting saws and forklifts whisking boxes to and fro.

Pregnant, the stench was especially difficult for Lola to stomach. She pulled a handkerchief from her purse and covered her mouth and nose. They both shuddered at the cold temperatures of the well refrigerated plant. Approaching a burly mustached man donning a bloodied white smock, they asked him where they could locate Doug Reynolds. "You won't catch him on the floor," said the man. He directed them to a stairwell toward the rear which led to the offices above.

They ascended the stairs and reached an office. Savoy knocked on the thin glass of an office door on the second floor and a male voice yelled out telling them to enter. Doug, who was seated behind a desk littered with blueprints and binders of documents asked rather nonchalantly, "Can I help you?"

"Mr. Reynolds, my name is Savoy Graves, and this is my wife Lola. We called earlier about meeting with you." Barely raising his eyes to meet the couple, Doug replied, "Yes, I only have a few minutes to spare. How can I help you?"

They proceeded to explain their purpose and began to ask him a series of questions about his time at Thornwood Manor and his relationship with the workforce, and particularly with Barry Gribbon. Doug explained how he was awarded the contract to construct and monitor the power plant at the facility. "I am damn proud of that work," he announced. "The plant still stands today." He explained that he ran the facility like he did with all places under his control. "I was a no-nonsense kind of guy." Doug explained that he didn't have much recollection of the lower-level employees at Thornwood, though Barry's name did ring a bell.

Savoy then asked if he recalled the death of Adeline Deveraux in 1977. Doug paused for a moment and replied, "It was a psychiatric facility. My guess is that sort of thing happened a lot. I was only responsible for operating the power plant."

Savoy persisted, "We had heard that there was an incident where Barry reportedly harassed Adeline. Any recollection of that? Perhaps you have some employment records we can review?"

Doug nodded his head before stating, "I'm a busy guy who has always been in high demand. I never have time for minor details that occur outside of my operation."

They looked crossly at him. The death of a young girl was not minor, certainly not to them.

Sensing their displeasure, Doug continued in a softer tone, "Look," he said, "I really don't have any information that could be of help. That was many years ago, and I no longer have any records from Thornwood. I wish I did. I'm sorry. All I can tell you is the last I heard about Barry was he landed a job at Mercy Hospital in Westchester. When they called for a reference, I almost told them that my impression of him was that he was never much of a mechanic, but I figured that would be their problem, not mine."

Savoy scribbled the information into his notebook. He then glanced at Lola before reaching into his pocket to retrieve a copy of the image that Elena had found on the floor of Adeline's room the day she died.

"We understand you are a busy man," said Savoy, "and we appreciate the value of your time, so we just have one more question for you." He held out the image in the photograph of the stags. "Do you recognize this?"

Doug studied the image for a moment. "What on earth is this?" he asked with a puzzled expression.

"There was a card found at the scene with this image on it," Savoy replied as he reached out to retrieve the sketch from Doug. They rose and thanked Doug for his time.

As they made their way down the stairs and quickly exited the plant, Lola rolled her eyes and said, "What a pompous ass. And what about that comment about minor details? He sounds like an insensitive prick."

"Unbelievable," replied Savoy. "But at least he gave us some helpful information. Let's head to Westchester and try to track down this guy Barry."

Unbearable

Thomas Deveraux sat in a lonely bar in Suffern, New York mourning the death of his daughter, Adeline, who was recently found hanging in her room in Thornwood Manor Psychiatric Center from an apparent suicide. Choking back tears, he reflected on his feelings, most of which were misguided hate. He hated that his daughter had a condition that a man of his intellect was not equipped to grapple with. He loved his daughter, but instead of empathy, her condition spawned a maniacal mixture of paranoia and helplessness within him. He also hated that his wife was not strong enough to challenge his fateful decision to have Adeline committed in the first place. If she could have pushed back, just a tiny bit, he thought, things may have been different. He knew he was wrong to blame them for these things, but he could not escape his feelings. He knocked back another shot of Jack Daniels and took a long drag from his cigarette.

Thomas had spent most of his life as a laborer. He was a hard but simple man. When he first learned that his wife was pregnant, he swore to protect and provide for his family. Although his wife's family had some wealth, his pride was too great to have relied upon it. Instead, he did what he had always done: worked longer hours to make ends meet. Upon learning of Adeline's diagnosis, he was confused. After all, doctors didn't know much about her condition so there was little that he could expect from them. As she aged, he saw her mature into a beautiful young woman, but possessed the mind of a child. Men also began to notice her. This was compounded by Adeline's overfriendliness which he feared would lead to unwanted advances from strangers that she was not mentally or physically equipped to handle. This did not sit well with Thomas, and instead of working with his wife to properly nurture and educate his daughter, he turned inward and blamed her for not knowing better. As a result, Adeline was forbidden from having male friends: a rule that she was not equipped to abide by. One day, Adeline was caught by her father kissing a boy several years older than her. This enraged him and the boy barely escaped his wrath. Thomas gulped another shot of whiskey and waved rudely to the bartender to refill the glass.

Thomas found himself staring at his own reflection in the mirror behind the bar. He hated what he saw and, most of all, he hated what he had done because it was a simple immutable fact that had Adeline not been committed to Thornwood—had he learned to be patient with his daughter and trust his wife—she would still be alive today. The fact that this decision was the direct result of her death was too much to bear. That, above all else, stung him the most. He was hurting inside and none of the other patrons in the bar, or anyone else in this world, except perhaps, his wife, could possibly fathom what he was going through.

Thomas took one final swig of whiskey, left enough money on the bar to cover the tab, and quietly slipped out the side door. He walked around the back, entered his car, and closed the door. He lowered the sun visor and a picture fell onto his lap. It was taken several years ago during a trip to the park where he'd carried Adeline atop his shoulders. She was clutching a soft teddy bear that he had won for her during a day they'd spent at an amusement park. She carried it everywhere she went as a young child. He focused on the bear and now realized it to be a symbol of their connection. He was not a perfect father by any means, but, at least for one day, he was the special guy who got her a special bear. He reveled in his self-pride only for a moment before relenting against his crushing guilt. In despair, he closed his eyes and began to sob loudly.

He then placed the picture on the dashboard and reached over to open the glove compartment and pulled out his .38 caliber handgun. Without hesitation, he placed the barrel to his right temple and squeezed the trigger. The bullet tore through his skull and brain, killing him instantly before exiting through the other side of his skull, shattering the glass window, and finally lodging into a wooden shed near where he'd parked. The next morning the body of Thomas Deveraux was found by police slumped in his car. He was pronounced dead at the scene from a self-inflicted gunshot wound to the head.

Loading Dock

Barry paced frantically on the loading dock at the rear of small hospital in Westchester where he worked. His afternoon coffee break was consumed by thoughts of this morning's encounter with Savoy and Lola who had visited him at the hospital to ask questions about the death of a girl at Thornwood Manor many years ago. His mind was racing. He could not understand why they would seek information from him, but they persisted.

Savoy and Lola explained that Adeline's death was ruled a suicide, but they were just following up on the case at the request of her elderly mother. They further explained that after searching his work history at the power plant, they learned that he was the only employee working the night before she was found dead. The couple probed into his knowledge of Adeline and whether he had a relationship with her. They even asked about an "incident" where he reportedly harassed her, and other questions, mostly general in nature.

Barry denied any knowledge of her death, explained that Thornwood was a very large facility with many employees who worked around the clock. Most of all, he strived to remain calm. The last thing he wanted was to arouse any suspicion about his tenure at Thornwood or anywhere else. Barry remained cordial and told them that he would let them know if he could think of anything that may be of assistance to them.

Just before departing, Savoy showed a copy of the Tempest logo to Barry. "Did you ever see this before?" he asked. They had both studied Barry carefully as he studied the image. Sensing their suspicion, he awkwardly scratched his right bicep, as if in deep thought, before saying that he had never seen it before. It was hard to tell if he appeared truthful or not, but it seemed to appear to Savoy and Lola that he was either unwilling or had nothing more to offer them. They thanked him for his time and left.

Although he had never been a Tempest member, Barry was keenly aware of the group's reputation. He first learned of them back in the fall of 1976 when he was summoned to Doug's office at Thornwood Manor for an employment evaluation. These evaluations were just a farce for insurance purposes and conducted to appease the state officials who oversaw the facility. Doug had no patience for such tedious exercises. Thus, there were no real questions asked of the employees during these evaluations.

As Barry awaited his evaluation, he saw a business card on Doug's desk with a unique logo. It contained an image of two deer stags with interlocking antlers and a cross in each eye. Barry, who fancied himself as an amateur artist, was intrigued by the design. When he heard Doug entering the office, he'd instinctively tucked the card into his shirt pocket. It wasn't until months later that Barry learned of the group's power, and over the years, he'd developed a strong admiration and fear of the Tempest group. The last thing he ever wanted to do was be involved with them in any way. Thus, he was very uneasy when Savoy and Lola had questioned him about it, and he naturally withheld his knowledge of the logo from them.

The fact that these strangers were *now* probing into his life infuriated Barry. In anger, he kicked a nearby metal dumpster and quickly recoiled his foot from the sharp pain. He peered up at the security camera on the loading dock and struggled to keep his composure for fear of drawing any suspicion upon himself. He clenched his teeth as he contemplated his encounter with the couple before conducting a quick internet search of Savoy Graves on his cell phone. Articles popped up about his recent involvement in a cold case on Long Island. Barry turned his head and drove his fist into a nearby box being readied for delivery. A co-worker witnessed this and asked, "Are you ok, man?"

"Fuck off," replied Barry as he drew the last drag of his cigarette before stuffing it into the cup of his half-finished coffee and tossing it into the dumpster. He turned quickly, and in frustration, returned to work consumed by thoughts of these strangers questioning his past.

Threshold

Savoy waited patiently outside a courtroom on the twelfth floor of the Eastern District of New York in Brooklyn. He gazed out the giant glass windows offering magnificent views of the surrounding area and bright beautiful sky. In the distance, he could see a plane flying back and forth lining the sky in a checkered pattern with powdery smoke. It did seem odd that it appeared to be the same plane doing this and he thought about Jonah's description of "chemtrails." Moments later, the large doors swung open forcefully as a team of attorneys exited the court. Dre followed behind, slipping papers into his black leather bag. "Sorry you had to wait, dude," he said with a flushed face. Having spent all morning arguing against a motion to dismiss made by a sleazy lawyer representing a drug trafficker left

Dre in a foul mood. "Judge Humboldt had no patience today and he wasn't shy about showing it," he said. Savoy nodded in amusement. His respect and pride for his law-school comrade was always reinforced when he heard about his work.

They sat down on a large marble bench overlooking the glass windows. "What's going on?" asked Dre.

"Listen to this," replied Savoy. "We've been chipping away at this and before we dig deeper, I want to bring you up to speed with our findings."

"Look at you vying to be the hero again," replied Dre.

"A hero is just a sandwich," replied Savoy with a smile. "I'm just trying to do what's right." Savoy removed a folder from his bag and placed it between them and began his presentation. "Okay, here's what we got. First, we visited the Rockland County Historical Society and got some information on Thornwood Manor. That facility has a long history. We found some pictures of the facility and employees during holiday parties and shows they put on, etc."

Dre listened while responding to an email he'd received on his phone.

Savoy continued, "Then we visited the actual site of Thornwood Manor. It was surreal just being there. Many of the buildings still stand, although they are largely vandalized and decrepit. We walked the grounds and even snuck into some of the buildings. We eventually found the old power plant and checked it out. Deep within the building, we found some old file cabinets containing log books." Savoy explained the operational purpose of the log books and that they were able to retrieve a log book containing entries around the time of Adeline's death. "I left the log book in the car, but, trust me, it's intact."

Dre remained attentive, but unimpressed.

Savoy continued, "We then visited the woman who took care of Adeline. She worked there at the time and was the person who found Adeline dead in the room." Savoy explained how Elena identified one of the employees in the staff picture as a man who had harassed Adeline on at least one occasion and that person, named Barry Gribbon, happened to be on duty in the power plant just a few hours before Adeline was found dead. He explained that they visited both Barry and his former boss Doug but were unable to get any useful information from those conversations.

Dre placed his phone down on top of Savoy's file and sucked his teeth. "You know our deal, right? I need credible, physical evidence. Everything you have told me so far is circumstantial, at best, and nothing to suggest any criminality. Hell, even if there was something to it, it would be a state crime and I only have jurisdiction over federal crimes."

Savoy nodded in agreement.

"What about police reports and autopsy records?" asked Dre as he scanned through the file.

Savoy explained that without a hint of foul play, the police merely questioned a few of the employees at the scene and otherwise rested entirely upon the medical examiner's report which deemed the death a suicide. "Look," Savoy said with growing desperation, "I know the deal: you need credible, physical evidence but I was hoping that you could run a check into this guy, Barry. Maybe he has a criminal record. We need something we can build from."

Dre looked at Savoy for a long moment. He always admired his friend's diligence and compassion, but he worried that he was wasting his time on this case. Rather than share his grim view, he resumed his study of the file, hoping to find something that may prompt more questions. Then he came upon the image captured by Elena within the folder. He held it up toward to glass to get a thorough look. "Where did you get this?" he asked. Savoy explained that Elena took a picture of the business card on the floor in Adeline's room the day she was found dead. "A so-called expert with knowledge of the dark underworld told us that it may have something to do with a secret society called the Tempest," said Savoy with a hint of amusement.

The drawing commanded Dre's full attention, fueling Savoy's anxiety. "Do you know anything about it?" he asked. "Maybe" Dre replied as he snapped a picture of the drawing with his phone before placing it back in his file. "Look," he said. "I will see what I can do. We'll run a check to see if this guy, Barry, is in the system. No promises, but I will let you know if I learn anything."

Savoy was pleasantly surprised at Dre's sudden change of tone and his agreement to check into Barry. He thanked him as they made their way down to the lobby of the building before parting ways.

The Ghost Orchid

Luis Abreu lived in a modest villa in Madrid, Spain. Despite his charming appearance and a 6' tall 180-pound athletic frame, Luis maintained a solitary lifestyle. He had never been married or had children. He preferred to spend all his energy on his work, which required extensive travel.

Luis was an enigma whose ordinary appearance caused him to hardly ever be recognized in public. He blended in with the crowd or, if necessary, escaped the crowd altogether. If anyone were to hazard a guess on the nature of his business, they would take Luis for a salesman, or a banker, or a barista in a sleepy coffee shop. His chameleon-like ability to be anyone or no one served Luis well in his profession. After all, Luis was a hired assassin for Tempest and the success of a ruthless assassin relied upon stealth and anonymity. For the last seven years, the group routinely assigned him the mission of eliminating former members who brought unwanted attention to their practices or outsiders who threatened the group's operation. Unfortunately, for his victims, business has been good.

Luis was raised in a modest home in a small village near Valencia, Spain, but he was not born there. Instead, he was born in a poverty-stricken area outside of Lisbon, Portugal. His family was the victim of a targeted assassination which left his parents and two sisters dead. The killer took pity on a young Luis cowering under his bed and brought him back to Spain where he was delivered to the household of man named Delgado, a third-generation assassin for Tempest. Never having children of his own, Delgado welcomed the opportunity to raise Luis as his protégé.

Luis benefitted greatly from this upbringing. He received a world class education and became fluent in several languages, well versed in literature, and an admirer of modern arts. However, Luis was not groomed to be a scholar. In fact, he was raised for one single and unmistakable purpose: to be an assassin for Tempest. He was trained in most forms of martial arts and highly skilled in all types of weaponry. When Luis reached adulthood, he had one final task to complete before becoming a full-fledged assassin for Tempest. That task was to kill someone very close to him. It is believed that in order to prove undying loyalty to the Tempest, one must eliminate the closest person to him or her. This, Luis accomplished without hesitation, when one evening he snuck into the room of his mentor and surrogate father, Delgado, and strangled him with his bare hands. News of this sinister deed drew great astonishment and praise from the elders of the Tempest. From that day forward, Luis had earned his place within the organization.

All professional assassins employed by the Tempest had their own individual codes and styles to accomplish their work. Some, like snipers, preferred to lie in wait just to fire a bullet from a great distance in order to make a "clean kill." Others preferred a more sadistic approach and tortured their victims slowly and methodically. And there are those, like Luis, who prefer a more intimate style of delivering an honorable death, one akin to hand-to-hand combat. He enjoyed using weaponry more suited to complete his missions. There was something about hearing the last breath exit a body, followed by lifeless eyes, that Luis relished. Thus, to accomplish his kills, Luis preferred using knives, daggers, and swords. The steel of his blades were sharp, clean, and always effective. However, for special occasions, Luis fancied a garrote. A two-foot long piece of metal wire fastened between two thin pieces of metal pipe was his prized possession and most effective killing tool.

Luis had one other signature trait that differentiated him from all other Tempest assassins. Prior to making a kill, he left a flower called a "ghost orchid" for his victim. Native in only marshy humid areas of Cuba, Florida, and the Bahamas, the ghost orchid is one of the rarest flowers in the world. The flower boasts brilliant white petals and often appears in the shape of a frog. They derive their name because they are typically found perched on trees suspended in mid-air giving them a ghost-like appearance. The flower is so delicate that it is nearly impossible to cultivate outside of its natural setting. It took Luis three years to locate a dealer in Miami who could keep up with his steady demand for such flowers.

The combination of its brilliant coloring, mystical appearance, and natural rarity makes the ghost orchid a perfect calling card for Luis. His intention was to create a mixture of amazement and apprehension for his would-be victim before returning a short while later to make the kill. After eliminating his target, Luis then plucked one petal from the flower: a token representing the kill he had made. It was a macabre reminder of his intimate, yet deadly, deeds. To date, Luis had accumulated nearly 100 petals, and he had shown no signs of slowing his frenetic pace.

Tempest had many hired killers, but none like Luis. To them, he was a natural born killer, raised to perform one function: to eliminate any threats which may undermine the group and their activities. Known among the Tempest as the "Death Dealer," he was efficient, persistent, stealthy, and fearless. He was without mercy. He could not be bargained or reasoned with and he certainly could not be bought. Once, on an assignment in Vietri sul Mare, a small village in southern Italy, his target begged for his life by attempting to bribe Luis. Three days later, the lifeless victim was found with $100 bills carefully sewn into his abdomen. It was uncharacteristic for Luis to leave such a vulgar display, but the victim's bribery attempt had sent him into a fit of rage.

On this evening, Luis slipped into a dark apartment in a seedy city in Thailand to await the return of his next target. The unfortunate target was a man named Linus Young. Nicknamed the "Minotaur," Young was an exiled member of Tempest who was being aggressively pursued by the FBI and Interpol for his horrific activities in the production and distribution of child pornography. Few could dispute that the world will be a better place with the elimination of someone like the Minotaur. He was a monster of the worst kind who preyed upon, tortured and killed young children. Yet it was not the Minotaur's crimes that made him a target of Tempest. To the contrary, his crimes were widely acceptable to, and quite profitable for, the group. Instead, it was his arrogance that sealed his fate. Rather than remaining in the shadows earning his profits and paying tribute to Tempest, the

Minotaur went rogue and had been taunting law enforcement officials all over the world by publicly peddling his sadistic internet productions on the dark web. This had prompted unwanted global attention and the relentless pursuit of law enforcement. It is what drew the ire of Tempest and, ultimately, made him a target of Luis.

Brandishing his beloved garrote, Luis crouched in the corner of the dark room in a maniacal pose waiting for his target. Moments later, the Minotaur arrived, and when he did, he was not alone. He had a young child with him, woozy from drugs—and likely to be the subject of his next sadistic production. When the door closed behind them, Luis sprang into action with lightning-quick reflexes. He quickly overpowered his target and wrapped the garrote around his throat. Luis then kicked the back of the knees of the struggling man, forcing him to fall forward as Luis climbed on top of his helpless quarry. Luis braced his knees firmly against the Minotaur's back as he pulled the weapon upwards to tightly secure his body. With bulging eyes, the victim gasped for air while flailing his arms hopelessly. After a few moments, his struggle waned as Luis tightened his grip further to ensure the kill. With the Minotaur dead, Luis loosened his grip, allowing the nearly decapitated head of his helpless victim to fall onto the floor.

Luis quickly rolled off the Minotaur's lifeless body and sprung to his feet. He turned to the half-drugged boy whimpering in fear in the corner of the room. Luis approached, bent over to grab the head of the child, and placed one of his blades to his throat. The boy kept his eyes shut as Luis studied him carefully. Although he typically never left behind a potential witness, he was confident that the boy's dazed state rendered him unable to identify Luis. After a few agonizing seconds, he withdrew his blade and stood to leave. It may never be known why Luis spared the boy on this night. Offering an act of mercy was not part of his modus operandi. Perhaps he saw much of himself within the boy, or perhaps, and more likely to be the case, murdering him was simply an unnecessary part of his mission. The boy cowered in fear praying for Luis' exit.

As Luis approached the door, he retrieved the ghost orchid he had left for the Minotaur two days earlier, delicately plucking one of its petals, he placed it into his shirt pocket. He then used his cell phone to report that his mission was complete and listened for his next instructions. Without uttering a word, Luis took out his notebook and jotted down an address. He then left the building and went straight to the nearest airport to begin his next long journey: a trip to New York.

Summoned

Despite all his professional accolades and success, Doug Reynolds was never under any false illusions. His success was only possible through his affiliation with Tempest. It was their power that allowed him to land his lucrative business deals, including his coveted deal to construct and manage the state-of-the-art power plant at Thornwood Manor nearly four decades ago. It was their influence that allowed him to repeatedly cut through the regulatory red tape to land the permits and licensing necessary to construct and operate that facility and all his other facilities. This dark affiliation was also instrumental in keeping the labor unions off his back, which allowed him to hire a cheap, and poorly skilled, labor force while maximizing his profits.

However, Doug learned very early on that there was a price to pay for this relationship. A perpetual commitment to remain silent, obedient, and cooperative. There was also a duty to pay a monthly tribute to the organization that had helped make him what he was today. And now, as he sat awaiting a meeting with a high ranking official of the Tempest group—a meeting that had not occurred since he first joined this group many years ago—he was terrified.

Doug fidgeted in the brown leather chair on the third floor of some random office building in Armonk, New York. Up until now, he had never set foot in this building, but since being summoned there, he did not hesitate to appear. He carefully studied the décor of the dimly- lit room which had wood paneled walls, secondhand furniture, and boxes of documents strewn about. It was clear that whomever occupied this space was not who was meeting him today. This was far too simple and safe, and those he expected to meet today were far from that description.

The door to the office creaked open behind him. A slender, elderly man entered and took a seat at the desk across from Doug who sat silently and upright. The man stared at Doug, causing a shiver to run down his spine. "Mr. Reynolds, we have…a situation."

"Yes, sir," Doug quickly replied. "How can I be of assistance?" The man continued. "In 1977, a death occurred at Thornwood Manor Psychiatric Center. A young woman was found hanged in her cell. Her death was ruled a suicide."

Doug blinked rapidly contemplating his recent encounter with the Graves' who questioned him on the same topic. "Sir," he began, "there were many incidents that occurred at that facility over the years. My role there was to install a new power plant and provide the skilled maintenance staff for a period of ten years. I don't see how that…"

The man glared at Doug, immediately causing him to cease speaking and apologize for interrupting.

The man continued, "As I have said, the death was ruled a suicide. Unfortunately, and for reasons we have yet to ascertain, this incident is facing a new level of scrutiny. There are some who are beginning to believe that this wasn't a suicide and was instead a homicide." Doug listened intently, careful to not interrupt the man again. "This investigation is making the leaders of our group very…uncomfortable."

Seizing upon an appropriate moment to speak, Doug said, "Sir, please forgive me, but I do not understand. You stated that this was a suicide that occurred over 40 years ago. What can anyone do to alter that fact?" The man leaned back in his chair studying Doug. He obviously loathed even having to participate in this conversation, but he was compelled by duty. He leaned forward and said, "Mr. Reynolds, if you interrupt me again, I will have your throat slit from ear to ear. Do I make myself clear?"

Doug leaned back in his chair attempting to remain calm. He was terrified and could not fathom what may be required of him. The man continued, "Barry Gribbon worked as a maintenance mechanic under your direction at around the time of this incident. He is currently a suspect. If you have any information to share with me, now would be the appropriate time." A bead of sweat formed on Doug's eyebrow as he clenched his hands under the desk nervously.

"Mr. Reynolds. Thornwood Manor was a very lucrative investment for the group for many years. It offered us access to a vast amount of funds from the state, which greatly enriched our coffers. It also offered an excellent opportunity to move funds within our organization. So, the possibility of any investigation into that enterprise, even stemming from a suspected homicide more than 40 years later, is making a great deal of people uneasy."

Doug scratched is forehead contemplating his next words. "Sir, with all due respect, what is it that you need from me?" The man leaned in, looking more stern and said, "For the moment, you will do nothing. The purpose of this discussion is to learn any information you can provide to us and to make you aware of the situation in case anyone questions you about it. If that occurs, you will report it to me immediately. Is this understood?" Doug immediately nodded yes before the man continued, "Mr. Reynolds, you would be very wise to heed my instruction. Very wise." Doug stared blankly at the man. He contemplated informing him that he had already been questioned by Savoy and Lola but was too terrified to do so. In his mind, it was a harmless conversation and he had nothing to offer them. Rather than making things worse, he decided to withhold that information.

Doug assured the man that he would fully comply, and without saying another word, he stood from his seat and prepared to leave the office. At that moment, the door creaked open and another elderly man entered the room. Doug turned to the stranger, offering a meek smile as he exited the room. Just before he closed the door, Doug heard the man behind the desk welcome the stranger by saying, "Good afternoon, Mr. Walcott."

Reclamation

Bonnie Beacham boarded the 2:18 p.m. ferry departing New London, Connecticut heading to Orient Point, New York. The hour-long trek across the Long Island Sound is by far the most scenic route to reaching her childhood home in Farmingville. The ride on the ferry also gave her a chance to stretch after the long drive from her home in Salem, Massachusetts. More importantly, it gave her time to reflect on the passing of her dear father, who had died in his sleep yesterday morning.

Bonnie hadn't been back to New York since being fired from her job at the Rockland County Medical Examiner's Office in 1977. It was an occurrence that has haunted her, personally and professionally, and the long absence did nothing to quell her disdain over that fateful event. As the ferry passed a small lighthouse, she recalled many summers spent on this body of water with her father. He was a good man who did his best to raise his daughters after the death of their mother. He also lived up to his word by providing Bonnie with a solid education, if she kept her grades up, which she did. She graduated with honors, became a well-trained forensic pathologist and landed a dream job, only to have it cruelly snatched away by her unruly boss, Martin Walcott.

Bonnie never truly recovered from her time under Walcott's employ. She recalled the stuffy office and tokens of masculinity aimed at reinforcing the notion that, under him, it was a man's job and *only* a man's job. From the moment she began working there, Bonnie was unfairly scrutinized for everything. She made the effort to be extra diligent, just to be sure that her superiors would find her work satisfactory. She quickly learned, however, that it was not her work at all that was under scrutiny: it was her gender.

Aside from the personal pain, her departure from Walcott's office also placed a great strain on Bonnie's efforts to find gainful employment elsewhere. It was already difficult for a young upstart medical examiner to explain a sudden departure from the office led by a man of Walcott's reputation. Of course, it was fully compounded when Walcott assured her that he would do everything in his power to shun her reputation. This forced Bonnie to find work in smaller cities.

Eventually, Bonnie was able to find work in the suburbs of Philadelphia, Connecticut, and then Rhode Island. At one point, and to make ends meet, she had to change her careers altogether and began working in the medical records and document retention industry. The work was steady, but she was never able to recapture that "dream" job: one that, to her, signified that she had lived up to the bargain she'd made with her father.

Although Bonnie never married, she does have a daughter named Vanessa from a previous relationship who, in her early thirties, works as a travel planner for a local agency that plans exotic Asian and European vacations. Unlike her mother, Vanessa never had dreams of attending college. Instead, she set her sights on the travel industry, eventually making it her life's goal. Due to the nature of her work, Vanessa works abroad for six months a year, leaving Bonnie alone in Salem, often missing her daughter. Now in her mid-60's, Bonnie is semi-retired, but works part time in a medical examiner's office in the outskirts of Salem. However, she will be forever haunted by the personal and professional ruin inflicted upon her by one man: Martin Walcott.

The ferry captain announced the approach to their destination. Bonnie paused, allowing other passengers time to enter their cars. She was certainly in no rush. As Bonnie drove off the ferry and onto Route 25, she was met by a sign which read "Welcome to New York." This caused a sinking feeling in her stomach.

The 50-mile drive west to her father's home gave Bonnie time to reflect on his death. He was a good man with a big heart who would surely be missed. Bonnie pulled off the expressway, turned onto the familiar block, and pulled into the driveway of her childhood home. She could see her older sister, Denise, outside, smoking a cigarette. The sight of her sister's sorrowful face caused Bonnie to cry. Their older sister had passed away two years ago from a stroke and they both realized that they were all that's left of their family. Bonnie exited the car as Denise approached. The two held each other in a long embrace. It had been some time since they had seen each other, and this was certainly the worst of circumstances. They entered the house and sat in the kitchen to reminisce about their father and review the funeral arrangements. It had been decided that there would be a one-day memorial service at a nearby funeral home and he was to be buried in a local cemetery alongside their long-deceased mother.

Bonnie and Denise shared a pot of coffee while reviewing random documents pertaining to their father's estate. There wasn't much. He had drafted a simple will whose terms left each of them an equal share of the proceeds from the sale of the house and all his property, which Denise agreed to handle after Bonnie returned home, and a small life insurance policy which named them both the beneficiaries. There was also a letter left for each of the daughters to read. Denise, having previously read her letter, exited the kitchen to allow Bonnie some to time to open hers. The letter read, in part:

> *Dearest Bonnie,*
>
> *I want you to know that I am very proud of you. We made a deal a long time ago that I would provide you with the best education possible and you would earn that education and do great things. My heart is full knowing that you have exceeded all of the expectations I have held for you and those you have held for yourself. Don't feel sad. By the time you read this, I will be with mom, and we will both be looking down on you and smiling.*

Bonnie wiped the tears from her eyes as she read the remainder of her letter. She appreciated his kind words but struggled to agree that she had lived up to her end of the bargain. She folded the letter and sighed about the loss of her father before finishing the rest of her coffee.

Denise rejoined her sister. "I know," she said. "It's really sad."

Bonnie fought back more tears as the two hugged each other for a few moments.

"Go get some rest," said Denise. We have a long day tomorrow."

Bonnie nodded in agreement and went upstairs to take a shower before retiring to her childhood bedroom. She was physically and mentally drained.

The next morning, Bonnie lay awake in bed stubbornly refusing to greet the day, but she knew she had to. She eventually got up, showered, and dressed for the funeral. Denise arrived and they drove to the funeral home together. The two comforted each other as they entered to see their father lying peacefully in a simple coffin. He wore a black suit and yellow tie.

"He looks good," Bonnie said.

"From your experience, you would know best," replied Denise.

Bonnie smiled at her sister's obvious attempt at humor. "Good one," she replied as she leaned in to place her head on Denise's shoulder.

After the services, they made their way to the nearby cemetery. A priest led the group in prayer and a short while later, her father's coffin was lowered into a freshly dug grave.

Bonnie gently tossed in a rose and softly said, "Bye, Daddy."

They both thanked the guests who had attended the service and headed back to the house.

"I have errands to run, will you be okay?" asked Denise as she pulled into the driveway.

Bonnie nodded yes and watched her sister drive off. Inside, the silence was deafening, and Bonnie struggled to keep busy. After cleaning up the kitchen, she reread her father's note. Within the letter, her father explained that he had neatly organized her belongings in the basement. She marveled at how, even post-death, he was still helping her.

Bonnie made her slow descent into the basement of her childhood home. She hadn't been down there in over 40 years, but the stairs still creaked in all the familiar spots. When she reached the bottom, she immediately saw the rocking horse her father had bought for her so many years ago. She wiped some cobwebs off it and slowed pushed the seat, allowing it to rock. This caused so many memories to flash through her mind. She moved toward the rear of the basement and was greeted by the slight hum of the spare refrigerator. Although it looked worse for wear, the old frig was still working. She opened the semi-rusted door. It was completely empty; she mused how her father reluctantly allowed her to keep samples from cases she had worked on in the freezer of this refrigerator. Another remnant of the deal they each had made, she thought solemnly.

Bonnie closed the refrigerator door and made her way toward a large shelf near the back wall adjacent to the washer and dryer where her father had taken the painstaking trouble to organize his daughter's items into large boxes, each carefully labelled with their names. The meticulous nature of this act drew a smile upon her face as she recalled her father's organization skills.

Toward the right on the bottom shelf were two large cardboard boxes each labeled with Bonnie's name. She removed the lid of the first box to look inside. It contained many random items of her youth. She saw her favorite hair brush, loose photographs, including one of her wearing her favorite bell-bottomed jeans while standing next to her first car, old diaries, and other childhood items that invoked a great amount of joy for her. "Oh, Dad," Bonnie whispered as she marveled at her happy childhood.

Bonnie then removed the lid for the second box and saw items from her academic accomplishments. There were school pictures, diplomas, and other milestone achievements. She saw a picture of her with some of her friends at their graduation from medical school. The words "The tassel was worth the hassle" was written on the bottom. This brought back a flood of memories of her time in school and the commitment it required to achieve those degrees.

Inside the box was also a sealed package. The package, which had a mailing date of December 3, 1977, was sent to her home with no return address. She'd never seen it before, but then again, she hadn't been back to this house since she left so many years ago. Her father had always come to visit her. Bonnie opened the package and immediately noticed random case files from her time at the Rockland County Medical Examiner's Office. Even though it was a strict policy not to remove any files from the medical examiner's office, Bonnie often did so. It was her way of backing up her work. However, the fact that these files were mailed to her childhood home puzzled her.

She thumbed through the documents. Most of the files were from closed cases that she had worked on, but one file was from a case she had worked on but was unable to complete. It concerned the death of Adeline Marie Deveraux. She paused to recall that she was the young woman found dead at Thornwood Manor in 1977. She had long harbored strong suspicions about the death of that young woman, but she was never able to complete her investigation before being fired by Walcott. Bonnie then recalled her old theories of the Deveraux case, which had largely been forgotten by her over the many years since. After all, her work on that was the case directly leading to her being fired by Walcott and when she left that office, and New York altogether, any thoughts involving that painful experience were quickly and permanently pushed aside. Until now.

Bonnie tucked the Deveraux file under her right arm, placed the lid back onto the box, and returned upstairs. She placed the file on the kitchen table and poured herself a cup of freshly brewed coffee. She sat down and began to read the file. A suicide, she recalled, was initially believed to be the cause of death, but as time went on, she suspected foul play and began further testing. She recalled how she withheld her assumptions until the additional test results she had ordered came back. Unfortunately, she was fired before the tests were complete. Now, after 40 years, she was *finally* seeing the results of that testing. Bonnie compared her initial report to the results of the tests that came back afterward. She was stunned by what she saw. In fact, she was so engrossed that she didn't have time to catch the coffee cup which slipped from her hand and crashed to the floor. "Shit," she uttered as she quickly grabbed a dish towel to clean the mess.

Bonnie looked over the report one more time. She had to be sure. Once convinced of the findings, she picked up her phone to make a call. When the person on the end of the call answered, she said, "Solomon, its Bonnie. I am in New York. We need to speak. Can I pay you a visit in the next few days?"

At Wit's End

Savoy had felt demoralized since his last meeting with Dre. He knew that the investigation had yet to yield any information which would spring his colleague and his team into action. His fading hopes of ever discovering any foul play in Adeline's death now rested on an impromptu meeting with Martin Walcott. Their repeated attempts to meet with him proved unsuccessful, and it became clear to them that he had no interest in discussing the case. Now they waited patiently in the parking lot of a nearby convention center where Walcott was the guest of honor at a fundraiser. He couldn't avoid them now, they hoped.

The event finally concluded, and as they saw several people beginning to leave hall, Savoy and Lola rushed to the front entrance.

Fifteen minutes later, Walcott appeared dressed in a black tuxedo. He was flanked by several similarly dressed men. As he drew near, Savoy approached and said, "Mr. Walcott, it's Savoy Graves. I tried to reach you by phone several times. I wanted to speak with you about an old case you worked on." Walcott waved his hand dismissively and started to walk past them when Lola stood directly in front of him. Unable to avoid her, Walcott looked into Lola's eyes and she said, "Sir, it's about one of your cases at Thornwood Manor."

Walcott's face became flush as his entourage looked on. He collected himself, smiled, and told his group that he would stay behind to speak with these people. Alone with them, it was clear that Walcott was infuriated. "Who are you people?" he asked angrily. Savoy apologized for their somewhat aggressive behavior, but his repeated refusal to speak with them left them no choice. They explained who they are and began asking questions about Adeline's case. He stared silently with an indifferent look upon his face.

After a few moments of awkward silence, Walcott looked around before speaking. "Listen, Mr. Graves, I cannot help you. All the work performed on that case is in the autopsy report. And you, as an attorney, should know that I am not at liberty to speak about any case without a law enforcement or judicial warrant or to a direct family member." Savoy looked at him angrily and he attempted to explain that they had received permission from the girl's mother to investigate, but Walcott ignored him until his limousine pulled up alongside the curb. He waved to the driver before looking back at them and said, "I'm sorry that I cannot help you. Please do not bother me again. Have a good night." He then entered the backseat and nodded in their direction as the car drove off.

Savoy threw his hands up in frustration. "I can't do this anymore."

"What do you mean?" replied Lola.

"I mean, what do we have? We've found no credible evidence of foul play. There is nothing to suggest that it was anything other than a suicide. Nothing. And now we are busy chasing people around like the God-damn Paparazzi."

Lola, looked at him intently and, after pausing a moment to let a couple who'd exited the hall pass, she sai,d "Enough! This isn't the guy I have grown to love. That guy would never give up."

"Hon," he said in a calmer, but no less deflated, voice, "I love you, but I really don't need a pep talk right now. I am tired. We are tired. We are done. This is a dead end. I mean, what do we have? A young girl found hanging in her room in a psychiatric center in 1977; a former nurse who took care of Adeline who *may have* identified an employee who *may have* harassed her one time at Thornwood; and a freaky illuminati type cult whose connection to this whole thing is not even clear."

Lola stared at him incredulously and said, "Aw, look at you. You think you have it bad?" Savoy attempted to cut her off, but she would not be deterred, "How dare you? That old woman has it bad. She was forced to put her child into a psychiatric facility only to learn that she would die there. And now she is near the end of her life and may never know the truth. That is bad! Shit, if you had given up so easily in my mother's case, we wouldn't even be sitting here right now. Hell, we wouldn't even know each other. Spare me the sorry act, Savoy. Yes, this is hard, but don't make it harder than it is."

Savoy's anger was quickly replaced with admiration for his wife. He knew she was right. Of course, there would be doubts and frustrations. That is part of the process, but you must push past them. He recalled precisely why he needed her companionship and assistance in this case. Not just to help with the investigation, but also to control these negative thoughts and frustrations and keep pushing him forward. She delivered when he needed it the most. He took Lola by the hand and with a wink of his eye, he said, "How'd you get so tough anyway?"

The couple began to slowly walk back to their car in the near vacant parking lot now brightly lit by a full moon. As they reached the car Savoy's cell phone rang. It was Loretta Deveraux calling. Had she called just two minutes earlier, he would have ignored the call or figured out a polite way to tell her that they had nothing to show for their efforts, but he thought about his wife's sage advice. The poor woman has it rough and is nearing the end of her life. He owed it to her to do everything he could to garner information about Adeline's death, and if it meant that nothing could be found to change the result that she had indeed committed suicide, then she at least deserved to know that he'd tried. He showed Lola the phone to see who was calling.

With renewed confidence, he answered the call. Lola studied his facial expression which quickly grew more and more attentive. Savoy gestured to Lola to give him a pen and paper; she quickly obliged. He jotted down an address and thanked Loretta. He then said to the woman, while looking at Lola, "Don't worry. I promise that we will keep doing everything possible. I will let you know what we find. Thanks." Savoy ended the call and stared at Lola. He was aghast.

"Well?" she asked with budding anticipation.

"You are not going to believe this!" he said.

"Loretta just got a call from a woman named Bonnie Beacham. She was the first Medical Examiner to investigate Adeline's death."

Lola was skeptical. Until that moment, they had no idea that anyone other than Walcott had worked on the case.

"She told Loretta that she had found some information that may be very helpful. Loretta explained our involvement and she wants us to meet her and another medical examiner at his home tomorrow," he said.

Lola reached for his notepad to see the address. "Bainbridge, New York? That's upstate. Couldn't we just speak by phone? Lola asked. "I don't know, but it sounds important," he replied. "Besides, where is that person who talked me off the ledge just five minutes ago?" She smiled and asked, "Who is this other medical examiner and why are we meeting at his home?"

"She said that he was her…mentor," he replied.

"Huh," replied Lola, studying the address again. After another moment, she said, "Okay. Upstate it is."

The Green Mile

Barry sat erect in a chair in his manager's office with his hands folded. He was indignant. Next to him, his long-time union representative, Manny Davis, was sifting through the union contract in preparation for their meeting. Yesterday afternoon, he received a notice advising him to report to this meeting and was further advised to bring his union representative with him.

Over the years, Barry had received a growing amount of workplace discipline. In fact, it had occurred with such frequency that his coworkers jokingly dubbed his customary walk into the manager's office "The Green Mile"—a comparison to the movie where death-row prisoners walk the green floor to their doomed fate. On this day, Barry expected to receive discipline again, but he was not particularly sure why. Perhaps it was the fact that it was only midway through the calendar year and he had already established a poor attendance record. Or perhaps it was from a job he performed two weeks ago where he was dispatched to repair a leaking water coil used in a large air conditioning system. Once he finished his work and tested the system, the coils burst again causing more water damage to the floor below. Whether it was poor attendance or shoddy work, or any other matter, Barry accepted the fact that he would be disciplined at work again. To him, it was just a futile game of cat-and-mouse between him and his supervisor, Stephen Bellamy, whom Barry despised. The idea of being lectured by a man younger than him, with no real experience in the field, made his skin crawl.

Stephen entered the room and immediately sat before his desk. He opened his file and paused for a moment before speaking. Barry let out an audible gasp and rolled his eyes in disgust. "I imagine that you know why you are here, Barry," said Stephen. Without waiting for an answer to his purely rhetorical, and entirely sarcastic, comment, Stephen continued, "It has only been six months and you have already exhausted all of your allowable sick time under the contract." Barry remained silent, angrily staring at him. "And there was that job last week. I cannot imagine how you thought that it was good idea to pressure test the system without being sure that you properly soldered all the joints. Do you have anything to say for yourself, Barry?"

Barry remained silent.

Manny dove right in, explaining how, for nearly half of his absences, Barry had provided medical documentation. He then opined that the leaks from the coil may have come from different joints and not the ones Barry had repaired. Sensing that Stephen wasn't accepting any of the mitigating circumstances that he presented, Manny stated, "Look, employee discipline is meant to teach, not punish. Let the mere threat of discipline serve as the discipline. Barry understands that more is required of him and he is prepared to do better. He is apologetic and has been working here for many years."

Stephen removed his glasses and closed his eyes as he pinched the bridge of his nose. "Look, Manny, you are right. I am not here to give Barry a hard time, so let's just make this simple. I will issue him a written warning for poor attendance and equally poor work performance, and it will be placed into his file. If you wish to file a grievance challenging it, you may do so."

Manny thanked Stephen as Barry nodded, quite pleased at the efforts of his union representative who'd allowed him to escape far worse discipline. They each prepared to stand.

"Hold on," said Stephen. "There is more to discuss." This surprised both Barry and Manny as they looked at each other quizzically.

Stephen placed his pen down and looked at Barry intently before stating, "About two days ago, two federal agents came in asking questions about you, Barry. They refused to give any specifics, but it was clear that it involved some sort of criminal investigation. They did inform me that you have a criminal record. This prompted our own internal investigation, and, after reviewing your employment file, it appears that you lied on your application for employment with us when you clearly stated that you had no criminal record. As you know, lying on an application can be grounds for immediate dismissal." Stephen paused for a moment to allow them time to respond.

They were each genuinely stunned by this news and could offer no rebuttal. "Based upon this information," said Stephen, "I am sorry to tell you, Barry, that you are now suspended without pay, indefinitely, until we can review this matter with human resources and legal counsel. Barry, I suggest that you prepare yourself for an investigation from the

FBI. You should probably get a lawyer."

Stephen left the office to allow them some time to discuss this news. Barry stared wildly in disbelief as Manny began to ask him a flurry of questions. He nodded reflexively to Manny's questioning as he pondered his situation. He couldn't regret lying on his job application. After all, he had to withhold his criminal record from them if he had any hopes of landing the job in the first place. His real concern was how he could be the subject of an FBI investigation. He recalled his past convictions, but they were minor, occurred long ago, and shouldn't have drawn the attention of the FBI. None of this made sense to him.

A sharp pain began to form in the pit of Barry's stomach. He thought of his late father and how he was never able to make him proud. Here he was, much older in life and about to lose his cushy job at the hospital. Even worse, he was now the possible subject of a criminal investigation. His fear morphed into anger and, as is often the case during his fits of rage, Barry began to see red. He strained to understand who was responsible for bringing this to the attention of the FBI, and then, like a lightning bolt, he remembered Savoy and Lola questioning him about his time at Thornwood. He wondered if that had anything to do with this before he quickly rose and said sternly to Manny, "I have to go. I will call you when I find out what the hell is going on." He then went to the employee locker room and quickly changed out of his uniform and, without uttering a word to anyone, Barry stormed out of the hospital.

Balance

Savoy and Lola drove along the scenic Route 17 on the way to the upstate home of Solomon Vessey to meet with him and Bonnie Beacham. As they drove, Savoy reminisced about his friend, John Conte, who lived not too far from their destination. "Maybe we should stop by to see the old man," quipped Savoy.

Lola nodded her approval at seeing the man who had been so instrumental in Savoy's investigation into her mother's death and a guest at their wedding.

"Let's see how things go," said Savoy who wanted to remain focused. They stopped for a quick bite at the Rocsoe diner, a locally renowned eatery in Roscoe, New York which draws a wide variety of traveling patrons including truckers, seasonal hunters, fisherman and college students. Along with its delicious food and friendly service, the diner is known for being adorned with a multitude of college banners from all over the country.

Savoy and Lola entered the diner and sat in a booth toward the rear next to a large window overlooking the parking lot. "I'm off to the little ladies' room," said a smiling Lola who made her way toward the restroom. Savoy was checking his phone for any messages or emails when Dre called. He picked up the on the first ring. "Savoy," said Dre. "We ran a check on this guy, Barry Gribbon, and he does have a criminal record. It's mostly low-level stuff like solicitation of prostitution and some minor crimes, but nothing more." Drawing no optimism from these words, Savoy asked Dre if it was something he could use. Dre ignored the question and said, "Listen very carefully, my friend. The kid in the bookstore was right. That drawing you had in your file—the one with the two stag heads with interlocking antlers—that is the logo for a dark group called the Tempest. They are an international crime syndicate and have been on the FBI's radar for some time now." Savoy listened in disbelief. He was in shock to hear that a global criminal enterprise may somehow be involved in Adeline's death. Lola had returned and sat in the booth. He looked at her before closing his eyes. He knew exactly what Dre would say next. "Look," he said, "This group is serious business. They are suspected of committing a wide array of crimes, including murder. They're dangerous and very well connected. I have to urge you to stop what you are doing and end the investigation. For the sake of yourselves and the baby, this is not a group you want to tangle with." Savoy thanked Dre and abruptly ended the call.

Lola studied his face. It had fear written all over it. She asked who had called.

"It was Dre," he said. "Remember that drawing that Elena made, the one we brought to the bookstore?" he asked. "Jonah was right. They are an international crime syndicate called the Tempest. The FBI has had them on their radar."

"Well, that's a good thing, isn't it? she asked.

"I guess," he replied sheepishly. "Dre warned me that we should stop working on this case. He said that they are dangerous and well connected. When Jonah warned us, I didn't believe it. It seemed more like fantasy. But now that Dre has warned us…look, it may be time for us to wrap this up."

Lola asked if Dre told him anything else. "He said that Barry has a criminal record, but it didn't seem to matter too much to him. It's clear that their focus is on this group. That won't bring any closure to Loretta."

Lola pondered that thought before asking "What's the difference? It's better to have them looking into something rather than nothing. If this guy Barry is part of the Tempest, and they take them all down, then we did our job." Their discussion was momentarily interrupted by the young waitress who came to their order.

Savoy assessed their current situation. On one hand, they didn't have enough evidence to convince Dre to take action. However, if Adeline was indeed murdered, and the killer was somehow associated with Tempest, then Dre's pursuit of that group may or may not ensnare the person responsible for her death. They could continue with the investigation, but now there was a very real and pressing concern for their safety. If Tempest is as dangerous as Jonah and Dre believe them to be, then continuing with the case thrusts them into danger. Savoy studied his loving wife. He expected her to call for an end to the investigation and with the baby on the way, she would be right. But he could not escape the nagging feeling of his commitment to Loretta: that he would do everything possible to uncover the truth about Adeline's death. He was genuinely unsure how they should proceed.

Lola equally contemplated their situation. She knew full well how dangerous it could be to continue. After all, nothing could be worth risking their lives. But she also knew her husband. Despite his momentary loss of confidence after their encounter with Martin Walcott, she knew that the detective in him was in too deep and it would be next to impossible to pry him from the clutches of his forensic nature. More importantly, she knew how sacred it is for him to follow through on a promise. To stop now would be to go against everything he believed in, everything she had grown to love about him. "Listen," she said, "I have an idea. We're less than an hour away from Solomon's home. What harm can come from hearing what they have to say? If we learn anything, and I don't have much faith that we will, but if we do, then we'll turn it over to Dre and he can take it from there. Then we can go back to our normal life and you can let Loretta know that we did everything we could. Deal?"

Savoy leaned back in the booth in deep thought. Balancing the fears for their safety with his commitment to Loretta was a tall order. However, Lola made a compelling argument, and her courage inspired him, yet again. He wrapped his knuckles on the table and said, with as much courage as he could muster, "Let's do it."

Lola smiled and placed her hand on his just as the waitress returned to their booth with their meal. The couple made small talk while enjoying lunch as they each tried to conceal from each other their nervous suspicions every time a car turned into the parking lot.

Oblivion

It was a warm summer day and Adeline desired some fresh air. She informed Elena of her plan to stroll the grounds and the woman cautioned her to be careful and not to take too long. Adeline descended the stairs and exited her building. She passed several other stone structures that mimicked the building where she resided. The loud chirp of a cardinal flying overhead caught her attention. She blocked out the sun with her hand just enough to catch its brilliant red feathers. She came upon the large common building where patients would often congregate. Inside, people were seated sporadically throughout the hall. Adeline recognized some of them, but most were unfamiliar to her. Inside, two men were playing a rather fierce game of foosball. The loud clangs of the levers being swung aggressively caused her to bring her fingers to her ears to drown out the noise. These sounds compelled her to exit the building as quickly as she had entered.

Adeline turned a corner and made her way toward a thick group of trees near the far end of the property. The shade from the trees provided much-needed relief from the sun. She sat down on a small patch of grass to take in the scenery. Adeline spied several different types of birds. She tried to count them all but quickly lost track. Behind her, stood a large brick building she had never seen before. It possessed large glass windows in the front and a large smokestack towering over the building from the rear. With her curiosity aroused, she rose and made her way toward the large building. She came upon a narrow bridge that passed over a small creek. The sound of running water below drew her attention to the creek. A brilliant monarch butterfly flew toward her and landed on the bridge's guardrail a few feet from her hands. Adeline remained still so as not to disturb the insect, but it quickly flew away.

Adeline returned her focus to the brook and saw a path winding down behind the stone wall of the bridge, toward the water. The tranquil setting tugged at her eternal sense of wonderment and drew her to the brook . Without a care in the world, she slowly trekked down the slope to the brook's edge. She removed her shoes and placed her feet into the water. The coolness of the water caught her by surprise and she quickly removed her feet and placed her shoes back on. She then bent down and cupped some water with her hands and splashed it onto her face, bringing her immediate refreshment. She cupped more water and placed it onto her head. Beads of cool water dripped down the back of her neck, causing her to arch her back and shoulders. She did this several times, and, without realizing or caring, her shirt became drenched. She began to wring the bottom of her shirt to remove the excess water. She studied the creek for a few moments. The water cascaded through groups of rocks in varying sizes causing a steady burbling sound. She closed her eyes, breathed in the warm summer air, and felt as one with the creek.

Adeline was pleased to have found this new place and planned on returning as often as she could. It was tranquil and refreshing. It was a magical place where, at least for a short while, her sorrows ceased to exist, and she could block out the world. Fully refreshed, in mind and body, Adeline stood and made a slow ascent back up the path to the foot of the bridge. She turned back toward the buildings, rounded a turn and, much to her surprise, reached the entrance to her residence. Until that moment, she was completely unaware that she had circled the entire property and the brook was right behind the building where she slept. Realizing this magical place was near her residence brought her great joy. What she could not have known was that during the entire time she spent at the brook, right up to the moment she entered her building, she was being observed by someone standing on the other side of the bridge.

Preacher's Pond

Approximately 140 miles north of the former grounds of Thornwood Manor is the hamlet of Bainbridge, New York. This small picturesque town is situated near the Susquehanna River about 80 miles from Syracuse. Solomon Vessey lives in a large cabin home a few miles outside of town on a breathtaking plot of land containing a large apple orchard, with scattered pine and birch trees. As Savoy and Lola exited the car their attention was quickly drawn to a sprawling pond toward the rear of the home. Mr. Vessey and Bonnie exited the home to greet them. "That is called the Preacher's Pond," said Solomon, noticing their admiration of the water. "It's named after the former owner of the property who served as the town minister until his passing 15 years ago. They say it is a blessed and holy place. Me, I just appreciate its tranquility. Lovely, isn't it?"

"It sure is," replied Lola.

Solomon smiled and thanked them for coming and said, "Please, let me introduce myself. I am Solomon Vessey and this here is my colleague, Bonnie Beachum."

"A pleasure to meet you both," replied Savoy as they all shook hands before entering the home together.

Solomon was a short, stout man with refined features and a healthy appearance for a man in his mid-80s. He was a graduate of Columbia University where he later became a professor and for two decades served as a Chair to the school's Forensic Pathology program. Solomon oversaw the program while Bonnie attended school there and, unbeknownst to her at the time, he took a vested interest in ensuring she successfully completed the program. Over the years, he became a friend and trusted mentor to Bonnie. In fact, she would often refer to him as a second father.

Solomon had long been a leading national figure in the field of Forensic Pathology. Although his knowledge was second to none, Solomon never had aspirations of becoming a figure head in the politically charged industry. Thus, he turned down many lucrative offers to lead the National Board of Pathology: the agency that establishes the education and licensing requirements, along with formulating and enforcing the disciplinary procedures for practitioners in the field. The Board is also known for awarding very prestigious fellowships to esteemed members in the industry. Although Solomon had lent his valuable guidance to this group and other industry leaders, he had always preferred to focus on bettering the true practice of forensic pathology.

In his senior years, Solomon decided to retire and settle down in the bucolic countryside of upstate New York. Despite his age, he strives to maintain a healthy lifestyle which includes long walks and bike riding. To help stimulate his mind, he regularly submits written medical treatises and offers his services as an expert witness in homicide cases. Many defense attorneys attempt to undermine his credibility during a trial, but they have all woefully failed. Armed with a lengthy reputation, unrivaled medical knowledge, and passion for justice and learning, Solomon Vessey is revered by medical, judicial, and law enforcement officials throughout the country. It is little wonder why Bonnie suggested that Savoy and Lola meet with him to discuss Adeline's death.

Solomon escorted them to his living room and gestured for them to have a seat at a wooden table near a large bay window overlooking the majestic pond. "Can I get you anything?" asked Solomon. "No thanks," replied Savoy. "We stopped for a quick bite before coming up to see you."

Bonnie sat next to Lola and across from Savoy. She anxiously scratched at her fingernails; it was clear that she was eager to speak. They were similarly anxious to hear what they had to say.

Solomon returned from the kitchen with a large cup of steaming coffee and sat at the table, giving a Bonnie a nod, indicating he was ready to proceed.

Bonnie began, "Thank you both for coming. We invited you here because we learned from Loretta Deveraux that you are investigating the death of her daughter. What you may not know is that I was the first person to work on her case, and I recently came across some information pertinent to that matter. However, I wanted to reserve my judgment until I could confer with Solomon and allow him to also review the file so that he could offer his professional opinion as well. Please, let me start at the beginning."

Savoy and Lola stared intently at Bonnie who shifted her chair and cleared her throat before continuing. "I began my career as Medical Examiner in Rockland County, New York. At the time, the profession was obscenely male dominated by sexist bureaucrats prone to political corruption. Women, like myself, were regularly subjected to misogyny and unfair treatment. We were prevented from making any progress in the industry, largely because of people like my ex-boss, Martin Walcott. In fact, the only male figure who first began to support the industry's inclusion of women is the man sitting right next to us." This drew a smile from Solomon as she continued. "I worked very hard to establish my career and applied for a job at Walcott's office. They couldn't deny me the position, but my work was always subject to extra speculation and ridicule. Still, I forged ahead and performed my work in the way I was trained. For this, I was told that I wasted precious resources and was eventually fired for it."

Bonnie paused to sip some coffee as Savoy studied the woman. She possessed a unique blend of intelligence and passion which commanded attention. She was short in size, probably in her mid-60s with piercing brown eyes that radiated incredible courage and pain. It was clear that the experience of working in that environment had a profound effect on her life. Despite his immediate admiration for the woman, Savoy's was apprehensive. They just endured a very long car ride under the potential threat by the Tempest group. He hoped that it would be worth what these two strangers had to tell them.

Bonnie placed her cup onto the table and resumed. "During the morning hours of April 15, 1977, I was in my office when the telephone rang. It was someone from Thornwood Manor, a nearby psychiatric facility, calling to report the death of a 19-year-old female who was found hanging in her room. Her name was Adeline Marie Deveraux. I immediately reported it to my supervisor Martin Walcott and surprisingly he dispatched me to handle the autopsy." She paused. "Mr. Graves," she said, "The information that I am about to tell you is complicated but extremely important. We believe that this information will have a direct impact on your investigation."

Savoy's eyes widened with anticipation as he opened his notepad and reached for a pen to write down everything he was about to hear. Lola removed her cell phone from her bag, opened a recorder app, and placed the device on the middle of the table. He looked at her quizzically as she said with a wink, "You don't want to miss a word of this." She then turned to Solomon and Bonnie and asked, "Do you mind if we record this conversation?" They both nodded affirmatively, and Bonnie said, "Your wife is correct. You don't want to miss one word of what we are about to tell you."

Slipping

Every day, Loretta is accompanied in her home by several different health attendants. They are all friendly and caring. Today, Xavier Benson was assigned to care for her. He had done so twice a week for the last three years. Xavier is a large, powerful man with a soft voice and pleasant demeanor. Loretta often referred to him as a "gentle giant."

With her health failing at a particularly rapid pace over the last year, Loretta had been relegated to the first floor of her home. Earlier during breakfast, she explained to Xavier how she longed to spend time on the second floor of her home and asked him to assist her. He agreed to carry the frail woman up the stairs and guide her back into her wheelchair.

Loretta slowly made her way to the corner bedroom, which wasn't just any bedroom. It was Adeline's bedroom. And for many years she had painstakingly avoided it. Many times, she would pass by, faintly pawing the door with her fragile hands, but she usually avoided entry for she knew the pain it would bring. Nearing the end of her life, she no longer feared such pain, she embraced it.

She gently nudged the door open and looked inside. The bed was carefully made and adorned with soft violet pillows with Adeline's favorite teddy bear in the center. A white rocking chair with tan pillows was placed in the corner of the room. She recalled sitting gently in that chair in this very room many years ago, attempting to teach her daughter the fine art of sewing. Adeline had difficulty manipulating the needle and thread and continually pricked her narrow fingers. Finally becoming frustrated, she threw down the needle and gave up. Loretta soothed her daughter, explaining that some people have special gifts in certain things and others don't. Adeline played with some toys while Loretta continued sewing in the rocking chair and watching her daughter toe tap to Billie Holiday's iconic "What a Little Moonlight Can Do."

Loretta entered the room and inched toward the window. Outside she spotted a cardinal voraciously feeding from a bird feeder in the yard. She turned back toward the bed and recalled so many memories with her daughter. Her heart ached and she let out a sigh as she turned back to the window. The cardinal was no longer feeding from the feeder.

Downstairs, Xavier was preparing lunch for Loretta along with her afternoon dose of medication. He walked to the edge of the stairwell and called out to her. Hearing no response, he ascended the stairs and went to her bedroom. Not seeing her there, he walked down the hall and saw the door to Adeline's room half open. He entered and saw Loretta seated in her wheelchair facing the window. "There you are," he said affectionately. As he drew near, he could see Loretta's head slumped down in her chest. It was not unusual for her to take naps throughout the day, so he was unsurprised. "Loretta, wake up," he said as he gently placed his hand on her shoulder. Loretta was unresponsive. He quickly grabbed her wrist and felt a very slight pulse. He immediately called 911 and within minutes, paramedics entered the home and rushed Loretta to a nearby hospital.

Revelations

"To grasp what I'm about to tell you," Bonnie began, "you have to understand the manner in which I had been trained. I spent 15 years receiving a world class post graduate education. Within that rigorous experience, I was taught two basic tenets; the first is that a good forensic pathologist must always strive to conduct a thorough investigation. No stone can be left unturned. Yes, this can be time consuming. Yes, it can lead to scorn and ridicule by colleagues, but to me, the subject of our investigation deserves nothing less than an extremely thorough search for the truth. The second tenet I was taught, and this I credit to Solomon, is to always, always back up your work."

Solomon smiled at his younger protégé. She reflected all the positive values he strived to instill in his students.

Bonnie commented on the stressful environment working under Martin Walcott. Solomon chimed in to briefly describe the forensic pathology industry. "It is rife with politics and prone to corruption. Walcott has always been a political hack who cares more about his vanity than serving the public. So, the death of a young woman in a psychiatric facility within his jurisdiction was likely nothing more than an inconvenience to him."

Bonnie nodded in agreement and explained how indifferent he was when he heard the news of her death before nonchalantly dispatching her to handle the case.

"When I arrived at the scene," said Bonnie, "I immediately cleared the room of all personnel, except the local police, so that I could conduct a thorough investigation of the body. Out of an abundance of caution, I also asked that all of the contents in the room be preserved in case any of it would be sent to the crime lab for analysis." Bonnie then explained that she always conducted a complete rape examination whenever rape was suspected. "For that reason," Bonnie explained, "I always brought my gear with me in those cases. This included a microscope, test tubes with a tube rack, small capsules containing a desiccant, glass concavity slides, normal saline, and dry ice. I did this with the expectation of taking swab samples at the scene. That day was no different. The first thing I did was take swabbings for seminal fluid from the introitus and from various sections within the vaginal tract. I also took swabbings from her thighs, breasts, and, in the event of possible oral sex or sodomy, from along the gum lines in her mouth and from the rectum."

"I prepared two complete sets of these swabbings, one for the crime lab freezer, and the other for my own personal freezer. At the scene, I performed an additional swabbing from the vagina which I dipped into the saline in the concavity slide in order to isolate the sperm cells so that I could examine them under my microscope to see if they were still motile. Much to my surprise, I found active sperm cells."

Lola looked at Savoy. They both cringed at the casual nature of the discussion regarding rape and death, but they understood that this medical profession required a suspension of emotion if they were to successfully perform such work.

"You must understand," said Solomon, "this was during the pre-DNA era. To identify a suspected rapist, our examinations then relied upon the study of enzymes, such as prostatic enzymes, and blood groups. It is the enzymes and blood groups within these samples that can be used to either identify or clear a suspect of any wrongdoing. But they deteriorate very quickly at room temperature or when exposed to moisture. Thus, they must be frozen and maintained in a moisture-free state until utilized. They are also quickly destroyed by repetitive freezing, thawing and refreezing, which is what routinely occurs in crime labs when accessed for testing." To simplify Solomon's point, Bonnie stated, "Think of a Thanksgiving turkey. You wouldn't want to freeze it, then thaw it and then refreeze it again. The meat would get ruined."

Savoy scratched his forehead before asking "When you take these samples, can you preserve them for many years, or as in this case, from more than 40 years ago?"

"Yes," Bonnie replied. "First, I placed the swabbings in the tubes on the tube rack with the cotton ends up and ran my portable fan to dry them. Then I inverted the swabbings into the tubes, added the desiccant capsules to remove any additional moisture, and placed the stoppers onto the tubes. Then I placed the two sets of tubes into two separate, sealed containers, signed my name across the seals of each and immediately placed the containers into dry ice, which froze them for transportation. One set was sent to the crime lab freezer and the other to my own personal freezer where it remained pristine, because it was not subjected to repetitive thawing and refreezing. I had also photographed and documented all of this in my report in the presence of the local police."

"What happened to your duplicate specimens?" Lola asked. Bonnie smiled and said, "They were stored in the freezer of a refrigerator in the basement of my home." Savoy tilted his head back in surprise as Bonnie explained how when she first began working at the Rockland County Medical Examiner's Office, she had begun keeping duplicate samples from rape and murder cases she had worked on. This, she explained, was done to create a backup storage system where samples could be kept in pristine condition just in case they were needed in the future. It was another fine example of Solomon's training. Her father had a spare refrigerator in the basement of their home, and she convinced him to use it for work purposes. "If he knew what I kept in there, he probably would have said no," said Bonnie with a slight chuckle.

Savoy scanned the death certificate and medical examiner's report. The documents, which were signed by Martin Walcott, deemed the cause of death to be asphyxia from hanging, and her death was ruled to be a suicide. He scanned the remainder of the documents in the file before asking, "Why is there no mention of the samples taken at the scene?"

Bonnie looked at Solomon before saying, "We have discussed this and are at a loss to understand it. Reference to those samples should never have been omitted. Perhaps there was no suspicion of a crime. After all, it is always possible that the seminal fluid found at a scene could have come from a consensual sexual encounter prior to Adeline's death."

"But the patients at Thornwood were segregated by gender," replied Savoy. "We were told this by someone who worked at the facility."

"Yes, but that doesn't rule out all sexual activity. She could have snuck off with someone or could have even had sex in her room and then later died," replied Lola who then asked, "Is there a way to determine from the specimens when the sexual encounter could have occurred?" "Possibly," replied Bonnie. "The sperm cells were quite active, and I calculated the time of death to be somewhere between 5 a.m. and 8 a.m."

Savoy studied Bonnie and Solomon carefully. He admired the methodical and collegial approach in which they were describing this to them. He then added, "That would mean that Adeline could have had sex not long before she died."

"Yes," replied Solomon.

Savoy recalled Loretta's description of her daughter and a late-night tryst with a male did not at all fit within that description. He then recalled hearing about the encounter with Barry, who on at least one occasion, harassed Adeline. Thoughts of his possible involvement in her death began to grow, but he knew he had to remain focused on their presentation. He studied the file again and then asked, "The autopsy report states that she had died from a suicide by hanging. How does finding evidence of a sexual encounter in any way relate to the way she died?"

"She was intellectually challenged," said Lola. "Perhaps she felt jilted by a lover and, in a weakened emotional state, it led to her committing suicide?"

Bonnie looked at Solomon for a moment before leaning onto

the table with crossed arms. "Here's the thing," she said. "We do not believe that it was a suicide."

Savoy squinted his eyes and listened intently as she continued. "I arrived at the scene within one hour of receiving the call. As with any hanging, Adeline had a ligature furrow across the front of her neck which curved up behind her ears and disappeared on the back of her neck." Bonnie went on to explain that when the weight of Adeline's body exerted itself, the rope tightened upward on the neck and left an abrasion on her skin across the front of the neck just beneath the rope.

"Timing is critical in these types of cases," quipped Solomon. "You see, if the body is found early enough, and the abrasion still has a cherry red color, then we are able to perform a microscopic examination to confirm that the cherry red color is from hemorrhages caused from the abrasive force while the person was alive. However, if the body had been hanging for quite some time, the abrasion will dry and turn yellowish-brown in color. Then it would be of little use to a medical examiner because it would obscure the hemorrhages. Now, here's the key: if a body is hanged after death, the abrasion would be yellow-brown in color right from the onset and there would be no hemorrhages seen under the microscope. There is an additional relatively uncommon procedure, one that I have taught for many years, to assist in the investigation of hanging cases. You see, when the rope tightens across the front of the neck, it usually does not cross the carotid arteries at the same height on both sides of the neck. A good pathologist would undertake an internal dissection of the carotid area at the lower side because as it tightens over the carotid artery on that lower side, and if the rope was very firm, nonelastic, and with a considerable drop height, it would produce tiny hemorrhages on that side in the adventitial tissues—the delicate supporting connective tissues around the carotid arteries. Also, under these circumstances, it will tear the inner lining of the carotid artery at that location, and, if the person was alive, will cause tiny hemorrhages in association with that tear."

By the expression on their faces, it was clear that Savoy and Lola were struggling to grasp Solomon's medical verbiage.

Bonnie attempted to clarify by explaining how she conducted Adeline's autopsy examination. "Due to the suspected cause of death," explained Bonnie, "I did the examination of the chest, abdomen, and brain first. This drained her body of most of the blood. Then I carefully raised the skin from the area above the sternum up to the chin to conduct a dissection of the so-called strap muscles in the neck and the carotid arteries. I was searching for tiny hemorrhages in the strap muscles, the adventitial tissue around the carotid arteries and hemorrhages associated with any tear that I may have observed in the inner lining of the carotid arteries."

Savoy raised his eyebrows in complete bewilderment and tilted his head backward before saying, "Sorry, guys, I studied law, not medicine. What does all of this mean?"

Solomon peered at Savoy and said, "Savoy, let's first address the issue regarding hanging. With a rigid, nonelastic rope, and the significant drop height, one would have expected to find tiny hemorrhages in the locations where Bonnie had searched. However, there were none. And, even though Bonnie arrived within one hour, there was no cherry red abrasion or hemorrhages associated with the yellowish-brown abrasion below the rope on the front of her neck. All of this points to more than a very high likelihood that Adeline was not alive at the time of the hanging."

Savoy leaned back and scratched his forehead in astonishment. "If I understand you correctly," he said, "Adeline could not have committed suicide by hanging because she was not alive when the rope was around her neck?"

"Yes," Bonnie replied.

Savoy glanced at Lola who was equally astonished at this notion before stating, "So you are suggesting that she was killed, and her body was positioned to make it look like a suicide?"

"A person who is already dead cannot kill herself," Bonnie replied.

They were stunned at this revelation and a flurry of questions immediately came to mind, but before Savoy could speak, Lola quipped, "Well, then, how did she die?"

Bonnie replied, "Well, I did find tiny hemorrhages. This is a clear sign that Adeline was struggling to breath against an obstruction that may have been smothering her and, in doing so, small blood vessels in those muscles burst. Thus, I suspected that it may have been death by smothering."

"Smothering?" asked Lola.

"Someone likely placed a hand or object over her nose and mouth to asphyxiate her," Solomon said. "Without clear signs of facial bruising, it is almost impossible to prove death by smothering. Typically, we would search for petechial hemorrhages of the conjunctivae of her eyes, and in the linings of the lungs, larynx, and trachea."

"Indeed," added Bonnie. "I found petechial hemorrhages at each of those locations. After the autopsy, I also conducted a microscopic inspection and determined that the air sacs in her lungs were overinflated. I also found fluid and hemorrhages within the lining of the air sacs. This, in conjunction with the hemorrhages I found in the strap muscles, led to my conclusion that these hemorrhages occurred when Adeline made a desperate attempt to breathe against an obstruction.

I then conducted another inspection of her lips and found bruising from where her lips were forcibly pressed against her teeth."

All three stared intently at Bonnie, riveted by her words.

"Even with these results, I decided to conduct one additional examination for textile fibers. I found fiber samples on her lips, and inside her nose, larynx, and bronchi. Believing that this could have indicated what may have been used to smother her, I contacted the crime lab to compare those fiber samples with the bed linens in Adeline's room."

"Did that yield any results?" asked Savoy.

"I was fired by Walcott before those results came back from the crime lab," she lamented.

Savoy slumped in his chair in frustration. He and Lola so badly sought the incontrovertible truth about Adeline's death and hearing that it may be close, only to learn that Bonnie lacked these critical test results that could have led to that truth left him deflated.

"Savoy," said Bonnie who waited for his eyes to meet hers before continuing, "My father recently passed away and I returned to his house to deal with his funeral. I haven't been back to New York since losing my job in 1977, so you can imagine the emotions going through my mind. After the services, I returned to the home and went to retrieve some items left for me by my father. Inside a box was the file for this case. It was mailed to me sometime between my getting fired and my leaving New York for good. I don't quite know why, but apparently the file was mailed to my home." They watched carefully as she struggled to speak without crying. Even Solomon sympathized with his younger protégé. After a moment, she composed herself and said, "The fiber test results were also within that file. Those results were from the tests that I had ordered; tests that eventually led to the loss of my job, my home and my career. The results of those tests conclude definitively that the fibers found within Adeline's body were consistent with the fibers of the pillowcase that was found on her bed." Bonnie cleared her throat and raised her chin and said, "Savoy, based upon my professional opinion, Adeline Marie Deveraux did not commit suicide. It is my professional opinion that she was raped and then fatally smothered with the pillow in her room and her body was positioned in a way to make it appear that she had committed suicide by hanging."

Under the table, Lola squeezed Savoy's knee as he stared at Bonnie with his hand over his mouth, attempting to process what he she had just told him. Despite his exuberance, there was only one thing missing: the identity of the person or persons who killed Adeline. The only possible suspect that came to mind was Barry, but any information on him was circumstantial at best. Bonnie spied the dejected look that began to form in his eyes and said, "There is one more thing... Before I relocated to Salem, I arranged to have my duplicate samples transported to Solomon. He maintains the proper equipment to preserve them here in his home. Savoy, we have with us, here and now, the duplicate samples that I made during my initial investigation into Adeline's death. Perhaps this can help track down the killer."

Savoy thrust his fist onto the table triumphantly. Finally, they had some credible, physical evidence that Dre could use.

A more skeptical Lola asked, "Why is none of this information found in the official autopsy report? I understand that some of the testing came back after you were removed from the case, but certainly the other tests you performed should have been logged into your report?" Bonnie deferred to Solomon who held up the original medical examiner report in one hand and Bonnie's report in the other and said, "This is the original, albeit incomplete, report. You will notice that

Bonnie clearly referenced the duplicate sample kit on page 2, along with the tests she ordered. Just under her signature is the signature of Martin Walcott." He then raised the official report and said, "Now, look at the official report. You can see that Bonnie's information is omitted entirely and it was signed by—"

"Martin Walcott," Savoy quickly replied. "Do you think Walcott was involved in the crime?"

"We cannot know for certain," replied Solomon. "But we do know that he cared more about his career than performing the job to the best of his ability. We also know that he fired Bonnie for being exceedingly diligent on this case."

Bonnie, with her head low, raised her eyes to meet theirs and defiantly said, "At best, Martin Walcott was negligent. At worst, he was criminally involved."

Savoy slumped his shoulders and lowered his chin as he leaned back in his chair. The information he had just learned had taken such a toll on his emotions that it left him physically and mentally exhausted.

Lola was equally drained and no less amazed. Despite hearing the gruesome news that Adeline was in fact murdered, the validation that such news would bring to Loretta, no matter how horrifying, would likely comfort the grieving woman. As inappropriate as it made her feel, Lola couldn't help but smile. After all, not too long ago, she too had realized a similar validation upon learning the truth of her mother's death.

Savoy glanced at Lola and spied her reverie. He returned his focus to Bonnie and Solomon and said, "Listen, I have a friend, he's a federal prosecutor who works with a department within the FBI that specializes in cold case homicides. When I find critical information, I pass it along to him and, if they take the case, they will take possession of any evidence. Before we got here, I was afraid that we had nothing to provide him. Now, it appears that we do. I will contact him on our drive back and fill him in. We will get back in touch with you. If necessary, will you agree to testify to this information in court?"

Solomon nodded yes as Bonnie leaned in and said, "You're damn right I will."

Savoy and Lola snapped photographs of the reports and thanked their hosts for their hospitality. Before exiting the home and embarking on the three-hour car ride back, Savoy looked at Bonnie and said, "I was once fired from what I thought was a dream job. And when it happened, I thought that there was something wrong with me, that I wasn't good enough. Guess, what? I was wrong. You may not believe it now, Bonnie, but when the truth comes out, you will have your vindication. Everything you have told us today, and whatever may come of it, validates you personally and professionally. Your mentor is proud of you, we are proud of you, and most of all, your father would be very proud of you."

Tears welled up in her eyes as Bonnie managed to smile and thank him for his kind words. The sun began to set over the magnificent Preacher's Pond as Savoy and Lola left the home armed with this heart-pounding evidence.

"Where to?" asked Lola.

"Well, we had a deal. We go home. But first, it's time to contact Dre. This is big."

Conscious

The team led by Richard Ramos had seen a remarkable transformation over the last few years. A crop of newly graduated students flocked to this exciting department to take on the great cause of pursuing unsolved crimes. One of these agents was Phillip Moy. Moy graduated from New York University with a Bachelor of Science and immediately applied to work in a crime unit with the Bureau. He was young, incredibly smart, and possessed a witty sense of humor that had eventually won over the more seasoned agents on the team. Moy was assigned to conduct electronic and cellular phone surveillance. Title III of the 1968 Omnibus Crime Control Act is the FBI's version of wiretaps used by state officials for surveillance of telephone calls. With improved technology, investigators can coordinate with cell phone towers controlled by local phone companies to pinpoint a traced phone to within a square mile of its use. All calls are electronically stored in the agency's pen register, and Moy searches for patterns among the calls.

Moy's current assignment was to monitor the phone line of a suspected Tempest member. Most of the calls he had tracked had no distinct pattern. There were local, national, and even international calls made from the line. He compared the number of calls made to an unidentified number that he suspected to be from a burner cell phone and discovered that the frequency of calls between these two lines grew exponentially over the last month or so. Moy had previously notified Ramos of this connection, and with Dre's help, the agency was authorized by a federal judge to tap the line with the hope of capturing information on criminal activity. Moy had been patiently surveilling these calls until he finally got a hit. He sprinted down the hall, with papers in hand, artfully dodging personnel and office equipment. He finally reached Ramos' office.

"Sir," said Moy. "You may recall the warrant that was approved to surveil the phones of an individual suspected to be a member of the Tempest group."

Ramos, who was busy, offered him a nod of indifference. He was in no mood to be dabbling in tech talk with the young agent.

Moy continued, "Sir, approximately seven minutes ago, we traced a call made from that phone."

Ramos, who was now scribbling notes in his ledger book, failed to grasp Moy's urgent tone. He advised the young agent to take down the information and he would look at it later. Ramos turned to Haverstraw to inquire about any new leads in their investigation when Moy interrupted again. "Sir."

"Out with it, Moy," snapped Ramos. "I don't have time for bullshit."

"Sir," replied Moy, "pursuant to the nature of the call, I believe that the suspect was communicating with…someone on our task force."

Ramos dropped his pen as he turned to give the young agent his full attention. "What was communicated?"

Moy informed them that, during the call, the person relayed pertinent information that only someone working on this investigation would be privy to.

Ramos looked at Haverstraw and then back to Moy and asked, "Any leads on the identity of the person on the call?"

Moy sorted through his file and retrieved a document. "Sir," said Moy, "I conducted an analysis of the record, and prior to the sharp rise in calls between these two lines, there was one very brief call made to a number that is associated with a member of our team."

"Who?" asked Ramos. "Stuart Hennessy," replied Moy.

Ramos peered out his office window to see Stu seated at his desk, staring at his computer. As if sensing that he was being watched, Stu raised his eyes toward the office. Their eyes met. Ramos held the stare as Stu made a futile attempt to look natural and returned his gaze back to his computer.

Stu had long feared the day that he would be exposed. He was keenly aware of the technology that the agency possessed and, even though they agreed to use a burner cell phone, once he learned the calls were being tapped, the pressure had mounted, and Stu knew it was simply a matter of time before he would be implicated. He had spent many sleepless nights fearing his arrest. Would it be a raid at home? Or perhaps in the field? Or even worse, would he fall victim to Tempest? Deep down, he knew there was no escape, and although the exchange between he and Ramos was brief, the mutual intuition between the two seasoned law enforcement men confirmed Stu's guilt.

Stu rose and began to walk slowly toward the rear of the floor.

Ramos and Haverstraw moved toward the office door and Stu accelerated his pace before sprinting to the stairwell door. Ramos, Haverstraw, and three other agents sprinted after Stu who rushed toward the basement of the building.

The clerk at the evidence room in the basement met their approach with great surprise. Ramos raised a finger to his mouth, gesturing her to show them where Stu had gone. She pointed toward a doorway to the left of the evidence room. Haverstraw slowly pushed the door open and everyone entered the room with weapons drawn. There, standing in the corner, was Stu with his gun in his right hand pointed at the ground. Ramos yelled for him to drop it. After a brief standoff, Stu relinquished his weapon and hung his head in shame as he was taken into custody. As he was being led out of the room, Stu told Ramos, "I want to come clean. I will tell you everything, I swear that I will, even if it means my life."

With that statement, Stu felt a relief from the crushing burden he'd been suffering for the first time in many months. More importantly, the team had discovered that Stu was acting as a mole for the Tempest group.

Chasm

Savoy hurried home to enjoy a long-deserved home cooked meal with Lola. During the past few weeks, the two had eaten more than enough take-out and diner food. And he'd taken great pleasure in providing Dre with the information they had amassed. His team was now informed that Barry has a criminal record, a fact that he had repeatedly lied about over the years. Barry can also be placed near the scene of Adeline's death; he harassed her on at least one occasion; and federal agents were dispatched to Solomon's home to retrieve Bonnie's report and forensic evidence. This information, along with a Tempest card found in Adeline's room the day she died, enabled Dre to finally send the cavalry and open a thorough investigation. Satisfied with the belief that they had done everything possible in this case, Savoy could finally rest. He wanted nothing more than to sit with his wife and enjoy a quiet meal while watching a documentary they had long put off.

Savoy and Lola sat on the sofa with their meal set before them on a small table. "You know," she said, "eating dinner in front of the television will be a thing of the past when the baby comes."

"Of course," he said slyly with a wink.

After their meal and some discussion, Lola reached over and hugged Savoy. "We did it," she said with great jubilation.

Savoy's smile was tempered with thoughts of Loretta's failing health. "I only hope that it brings her peace. I plan to visit her tomorrow morning to give her the news," said Savoy.

"It will," replied Lola.

Savoy hung his head. He wished he shared her confidence.

"Hey, look at me," she said as she extended her arms to gently squeeze his head between her hands. "We did everything we could. She will be pleased to know that Dre and his team are now on the case. But, most importantly, she can rest comfortably finally knowing the truth: that Adeline did *not* commit suicide." Lola patted his leg before standing up to head toward the kitchen. "Need anything?" she asked. "Nope, I'm good. Hurry back so we can watch our show," replied Savoy.

Savoy leaned back absorbing Lola's words of encouragement. He knew that she was right, that they had done everything possible and, for the first time, he began to feel satisfaction. He recalled that same feeling after helping to solve the crime involving Lola's mother. Such resolutions bring about a deep satisfaction that warms his soul. These feelings are exactly why he does this type of work. It helps to heal hearts, and that is his true motivator. Savoy and Lola also agreed to donate a fair share of their earnings from this case in Adeline's name to the Ohr's Syndrome Foundation: a non-profit group dedicated to raising funds for the awareness, research, and treatment of Ohr's Syndrome. The prospect of helping others with the same condition as Adeline brought them each great comfort.

With the case behind them, he could now focus on Lola and the baby. Things could not be better, he thought with a smile. The sound of a broken glass in the kitchen disrupted his reverie. "You all right, hon?" he asked. There was no response, so he took a sip of his drink and stood to head toward the kitchen when he saw a man enter the living room with his left arm around Lola's neck. In his right hand, he held a long knife pointed at her abdomen. It took a few seconds for Savoy to process what was happening until he focused on the face of this intruder. Much to his surprise, it was Doug Reynolds.

Savoy's heart skipped a beat as the world around him ceased to exist. He had long feared that this kind of work would lead to physical danger, but he was not prepared to face that danger in his own living room, threatening the life of his wife and unborn child. Lola was filled with fear and rage; the former for obvious reasons, and the latter because she'd loathed Doug ever since they'd met him at his office, and he'd displayed such callous indifference over Adeline's death. Still, neither of them could have known that he would later threaten their lives. Lola let out a soft whimper as a wild-eyed Doug screamed in her ear to be quiet.

Savoy strained at how to handle this delicate situation. One wrong move would leave Lola and their child dead at the hands of this maniac before Doug would spring into action against him. For now, all Savoy could do was remain calm.

"Did you think this would all end well, you piece of shit?" said Doug. "Did you think you would just keep your perfect little life while you fucked up mine?"

Clearing his throat, Savoy said, "What are you doing, Doug?"

"Shut the fuck up," Doug hissed as he dug the dagger slightly into Lola's arm drawing a few specks of blood. "You just couldn't leave things alone. You had to snoop around about that young girl at Thornwood. For more than forty years, she was dead and buried. There was no bringing her back. And now I will be on the hook for her death."

As the investigation continued, Savoy suspected that Barry was involved in Adeline's death, and while he still may be a suspect, he never dreamed that Doug may have been involved as well. His surprise, however, was easily outweighed by the clear and present danger standing before him with Doug violently clutching his wife. Savoy knew he had to buy time. He thought back to his encounter with a suspect in his home on Shelter Island. He'd used psychological jujitsu to distract him just long enough from killing himself until law enforcement could barge in and arrest him. But the risk at that time paled in comparison to what he was now facing. Here, the lives of Lola and the baby were in direct danger, and if something happened to them, well, he didn't much care for what would happen to himself. Besides, there wasn't an army of federal agents waiting outside ready to bust in once he uttered some code words. It was just him and Lola against an armed maniac.

"Why did you do it?" Savoy asked Doug with a calm voice. The very question seemed to bewilder him momentarily as he adjusted his grip on the dagger with his right hand and his clutch around Lola's neck with his left arm. He then caught his breath, and with an eerily calm voice said, "Because I could, that's why! I ran that facility. I took what I wanted. And that girl was mine. Did you ever have something that you weren't supposed to have? We had a good thing going until she fucked it all up. When she rebelled, when she threatened to take down all that I had built, I had to silence her. There was no way I was going to let her ruin everything I had worked so hard to build. Even if anyone caught on, all signs pointed to Barry, an incompetent brute with a criminal record. He was the perfect patsy; an unwitting pawn to shield me from any suspicion. But once you got involved, I knew that it was a matter of time before someone would figure out who did it."

"You're a sick guy, Doug," Savoy replied defiantly. "Adeline was an innocent young woman with a disability, and you took advantage of her. You preyed upon her and manipulated her, and when she finally had enough, you killed her. How does that make you feel?

Doug paused to reflect on Savoy's words. He had been self-centered his whole life and, until that moment, he never truly considered another person's vulnerability or interests. Of course, his behavior during his ill-fated marriage and how he stubbornly refused to support his wife's career goals also came to mind. He quickly whisked away such reflection and said, "Don't try to get into my head, you little shit," as he tightened his grip around Lola.

Savoy remained undeterred. "Do you know how we got involved in this case, Doug? Adeline's poor mother is dying and ever since the day you killed her daughter she has been searching for answers. She knew that Adeline wouldn't kill herself and for all your ability to control a situation, you could never erase a mother's intuition. That led her to us and here we are."

Sensing a slight receptiveness from Doug, Savoy took the opportunity to change course and said, "Look, Doug, it doesn't have to be this way. I can get you help. You can testify and maybe get a break. They know about Tempest. Think, Doug. The FBI could use your help. If you provide information, it may be helpful to your case. It's not too late." Doug's eyes widened at the mere reference of the sinister group. "You think you know about Tempest," he said. "You have no idea about them. You expose them and you're dead. Period. It's just a matter of time."

The inherent danger involved in these types of investigations were never lost upon Savoy or Lola. They each knew that trouble could arise, and they had to be ready. Savoy had been taking Capoeira classes and was quite pleased with his newly developed agility. For her part, Lola always went to great lengths to maintain a healthy lifestyle, especially during her pregnancy. They each knew that action may one day be required, but nothing could have ever prepared them for this situation. Savoy bought them a bit of time, but Doug was growing frustrated and impatient, and no one was coming to save them. It would not be long before he would act, so Lola knew it was time to make a move. She glared at Savoy, whose eyes were fixed on Doug as he continued to plead with him. The crushing weight of her stare eventually commanded his attention and his eyes met hers. With the mental connection established, Lola winked: an unmistakable cue telling him that she was about to spring into action. Savoy calculated the situation. Although he stood a mere eight feet from the brute clutching his pregnant wife, he may as well have been eight miles away. It was an unbridgeable chasm against a maniac wielding a knife a few centimeters from her abdomen. He needed more time, but his telepathic pleas for Lola to wait were futile. It was now or never and they both knew it. Lola was ready, even if he wasn't.

Lola subtly shifted her weight to ensure that she had proper balance, then slightly slumped her right shoulder before quickly raising her right elbow up levelling it into Doug's face, striking him in the bridge of the nose. The impact caused an immediate explosion of blood from his face, forcing him to loosen his chokehold. Savoy lunged toward Doug. Lola dipped downward toward the left but was unable to avoid his blade which pierced her stomach. Lola let out a scream as she spun off to the side while Savoy charged, knocking Doug back onto the couch.

Wiping blood from his nose and eyes, Doug tried to regain his senses as he battled fiercely with Savoy who stood over him, using both hands, attempting to seize the weapon. Doug pushed back until he was able to stand. He then raised his knee into Savoy's groin once, and then again, causing a sharp pain throughout his body. Doug partially relinquished control of the blade to use his left hand repeatedly punching Savoy in the back of the head. With stars in his eyes, Savoy could feel himself slipping toward unconsciousness. He glanced toward a weeping Lola on the floor, holding her stomach with a pool of blood puddling beneath her. This sight caused a surge of adrenaline to course through his body.

Armed with a renewed vigor, Savoy returned his gaze toward Doug who was now beginning to overtake him for control of the knife. Doug pushed Savoy away from him. Then with all the courage and strength he could muster, Savoy raised his right knee into Doug's stomach, and using his weight to gain momentum, he leaned back and flipped his assailant over his body onto the floor behind him. It was a classic self-defense maneuver that he'd practiced many times in Capoeira class. In the process, Savoy inadvertently released the dagger. He was unsure if Doug still had the blade until he turned and saw him regain his balance still clutching the weapon.

Doug wiped the excess blood from his face and offered a primal smile as he stood, tilted his head and prepared to charge. This was it, Savoy thought. They are all going to die here today, but if they were, it was not going to happen without a fight. Savoy quickly glanced around in a desperate attempt to retrieve an item—anything that can be used as a shield to repel against Doug's charge. Savoy grabbed a nearby lamp, ripped its cord from the socket and readied himself. Doug tilted his head downward, let out a grunt, and began his charge. He took two steps toward Savoy when a loud gunshot rang out. A bullet entered Doug's left shoulder violently spinning him backward into the wall. He tried to regain his balance until a second bullet tore into his chest, knocking him down for good. Savoy turned to see the source of the gunfire. There, at the foot of the doorway, was his trusted neighbor, Stanley, holding a pistol with smoke exiting the barrel. Unable to move, Doug coughed up blood and looked up at Savoy before drawing his final breath. Savoy immediately dove onto the floor to tend to Lola who was slowly slipping out of consciousness.

Loose End

A squad of federal agents stealthily approached Barry's front door armed with a large barricade. Since he was a suspected Tempest member, they left nothing to chance. On the count of three, they smashed the door, ripping it off its hinges, leaving shards of exploded wood on the floor below. With automatic weapons drawn, they entered shouting, "FBI. Get down on the ground!" They aimed their laser sights directly at Barry, who was seated on the sofa in the living room, quickly lowering their weapons after realizing his lifeless body posed no threat. Barry's throat had been slit from ear to ear and a puddle of blood stained the sofa and the floor beneath him. The agents sealed the area and conducted a thorough investigation.

A detailed search of Barry's home found a cache of pornographic movies and downloaded images of child pornography on his computer. Several guns, a large bowie knife, and a sword were also retrieved. Inside a closet, investigators found a shoebox containing Polaroid pictures of teenage girls some taken many years ago while he worked at Thornwood Manor. Several of them included rather innocuous photographs of Adeline Marie Deveraux taken at random locations.

Savoy had provided Dre's team with pertinent information regarding Barry's suspected involvement in the rape and murder of Adeline, leaving him as the prime suspect. It was of little consequence to him as his lifeless body sat in his living room with his neck cut so deeply that he was nearly decapitated. Ramos immediately called Dre to inform him of Barry's death and advised him to let Savoy know as well.

After a thorough analysis, the team discovered that the sperm samples preserved by Bonnie did not match Barry's DNA, thus officially clearing him of the crime. Inspectors then investigated Barry's death. There were no clues which might indicate who had killed him, but it was clear that it was a professional job. The only oddity, the one thing that seemed out of place and not in sync with Barry's lifestyle, was a delicate flower found in his apartment. A careful analysis of the flower by the crime lab revealed it to be a very rare ghost orchid.

Based upon their findings, investigators concluded that Barry Gribbon was likely targeted and eliminated by a Tempest operative. It is believed that he may have possessed incriminating information about the group, and with so much evidence suggesting his culpability in Adeline's death, it was just a matter of time before he would be picked up for questioning. In the end, he was deemed as nothing more than a loose end and properly disposed of by the group.

Stay with Me

Lola struggled to maintain consciousness as she lay on a stretcher being transported by ambulance to Winthrop hospital in nearby Mineola. Two paramedics worked frantically to address her wound as Savoy kneeled next to her holding her hand. Her eyes darted around the vehicle, desperately searching for relief. She could not tell how badly she had been stabbed, or more importantly, how deeply. The worry on Savoy's face did nothing to console her. She looked down toward her belly and the sight of her blood-soaked clothing made her sob uncontrollably. It was bad and they both knew it. One paramedic leaned in and urged her to hang in there.

Within minutes, they pulled into the emergency room parking lot, and the paramedics wasted no time removing her from the ambulance.

A team of doctors and nurses greeted them at the entrance. Savoy jumped out after them and caught a quick glimpse of Dre who stood off to the side. No words were necessary to convey Savoy's concern. Not only was the baby's life in jeopardy, but Lola's life hung in the balance as well.

They immediately wheeled the stretcher into the hospital. Lola's mouth and nose were covered with a large oxygen mask. Her eyes were swollen with tears. She remained fixated on the lights above her as they wheeled her in for emergency surgery. A strong sedative was administered and the last thing she saw before closing her eyes was her teary-eyed husband right by her side.

Savoy sat nervously in the emergency room waiting area. His hands and shirt were soaked in blood. Thoughts of a life without Lola and their unborn child ran wildly through his mind. He nearly vomited.

Dre returned with a bottle of water for his nervous friend.

"What the hell happened? asked Savoy. "All this time we thought it was Barry. We thought you arrested him."

"Check your phone," replied Dre. "I must have called twenty times. Our team went in to arrest Barry, but his throat was slit from ear to ear. I tried to let you know."

"Right. Sorry. Obviously, we were preoccupied," replied Savoy as he focused on the blood on his hands again.

"Hey, listen," said Dre, "Why don't you get yourself cleaned up? When Lola gets out of surgery you can't see her like this."

Savoy stared at Dre. He appreciated his confidence at her well-being. He only wished he could be as confident. Instead he felt fear, sorrow, and anger, mostly at himself for putting his family in danger.

"You warned me about this, Dre," Savoy said, nearly breaking into tears.

Dre shook his head and replied, "Get that guilt out of your head. You were just following your heart and so was Lola. You know damn well that she would be saying the same thing right now. You did well, my friend. And don't worry, everything is going to be just fine."

Both men stood and Dre gave Savoy a firm embrace, repeating, "Everything is going to be just fine."

Several hours later, Lola awoke in an immediate panic. She looked down at her belly and gasped with fear. Unsure of what happened, she firmly gripped the sides of the hospital bed as Savoy leaned over her. She was afraid to meet his eyes because she knew that it would immediately reveal the outcome of her condition and, most importantly, the condition of the baby. She was not prepared to face horrible news. She blinked for a moment then mustered the courage to look at her husband.

Savoy was relieved to see her awake. He squeezed her hand gently. With a dry mouth and barely audible voice, she said, "What happened?"

Savoy offered a brief smile and said, "Remember when you said our child was baby-lite? Well, I think he or she is a lot stronger than that." Lola closed her eyes. She had never felt such relief in her entire life. Savoy continued, "When Doug stabbed you, you twisted sideways just enough, and the blade missed your uterus by centimeters. You'll have a nasty scar, but I'm sure we can live with that."

Tears of joy sprang from her eyes. "You did it, Lola," said Savoy. "You saved our child and yourself. The doctors said it was a damn near miracle."

"I got him pretty good, huh?" said Lola referring to the blow she leveled into Doug's nose. "Damn right, you did" replied Savoy now smiling.

"Stanley...How did he know?" she asked. Savoy explained how their burly neighbor was preparing to bring the dogs back, but he wasn't sure if they'd returned home yet. He peeked out the window and saw the commotion before springing into action. He came in just in time."

"Just in time, indeed," replied Lola.

Savoy leaned in to kiss Lola on the forehead and said, "Rest, my darling. You need it."

"Stay with me," she replied while firmly holding his hand.

"Always," he replied.

With her mind at ease, and her hand gently caressing her belly, Lola, who was still groggy from a sedative, closed her eyes and fell fast asleep. Savoy pulled a chair close to her bed, placed his hand onto hers and fell fast asleep.

Tainted

Solomon Vessey took his daily morning stroll along the edge of the Preacher's Pond. He was in high spirits. After all, the information he provided to the FBI would be critical in helping to solve the mystery surrounding Adeline's death, which would bring about a measure of justice and closure for the grieving mother of that poor girl. He was also pleased to have aided in the vindication of his protégé Bonnie, whose professional career had been derailed long ago by his cruel nemesis, Martin Walcott. Although he should have relished in setting the record straight against his old rival, he was more saddened at how Walcott tarnished the forensic pathology industry and shook the public confidence of true professionals like himself, Bonnie, and so many others who had dedicated their lives to performing honest and diligent work.

It was a beautiful morning and today, as in most days, Solomon spotted several deer nearing the pond for a drink. His walks were so frequent and peaceful that he became one with nature and accepted by the surrounding wildlife. However, something spooked the deer and they darted off into the other direction foregoing their drink. That was strange, he thought. He had been as silent as ever. He continued his stroll around the pond and down small slope when he saw a person sitting on a large rock with his back to him.

Solomon approached casually. Many homeowners in the area frown upon trespassers, but not Solomon. Since his property abuts state land, strangers occasionally wander by and when they do, he always greets them warmly. As Solomon approached, the man stood from the rock and turned to face him. Solomon had never seen him before and had no reason to feel threatened.

Without warning, the man lunged at him with a sharp dagger in hand. Solomon was taken completely by surprise as the man jabbed his blade into his midsection, instantly piercing his right lung. He then stabbed upwards as he drew close to see the horror in Solomon's eyes. As he withdrew the blade, Solomon slumped downwards without making a sound. He was dead before his body hit the ground near the water's edge. His blood began to flow steadily downward into the Preacher's Pond, forever tainting its tranquility. The man went back into the home to retrieve a petal from the ghost orchid he had left for Solomon just two days earlier.

Reckoning

Stuart Hennessey sat apathetically in a federal court room in the Southern District of New York to await sentencing from Judge Helen Falick. To be sure, his prospects were grim. If he refused to cooperate, he could face the rest of his life in prison. His only real option was to plead guilty and fully cooperate with Dre and his team in exchange for a reduced sentence. Of course, Stu chose to cooperate, but not only for the obvious reason. He genuinely wanted to come clean and help them bring down the Tempest group.

Stu sat next to his attorney and across from Dre and several other assistant prosecuting attorneys. Collectively, they were all confident in the expected outcome. Stu could not share in their optimism. A heavy wooden door swung open and they all stood to greet the entering Judge

Falick. "Please have a seat," she said rather casually, "What have we got, gentlemen?" Dre and his team carefully set forth the evidence they had amassed about the Tempest group, the level of Stu's involvement, his willingness to fully cooperate, and the carefully-negotiated terms of the plea agreement. As part of the agreement, Stu would lose the pension benefits he stood to receive had he retired from the agency in good standing and was required to forfeit all of his property.

The Judge then questioned Stu's attorney who agreed with the terms that Dre had explained. She then turned to Stu. He lacked the courage to meet her eyes, but knew it was unavoidable.

"Mr. Hennessey," she began, "Do you understand the terms of the proposed agreement?"

He nodded yes, but the Judge needing verbal confirmation and asked firmly, "Please answer the question, Mr. Hennessey."

He meant no disrespect to the Judge. He was simply broken and struggled with his emotions. He cleared his throat and said loudly, "Yes, your honor. I understand the terms and fully agree with them. I make this proclamation fully and freely. I want to come clean."

"Mr. Hennessey," said Judge Falick, "In all my years on the bench, I have never seen the level of corruption and betrayal to the agency that I have seen in this case. While I am particularly loathed to sign an agreement that would allow the likes of you to escape all the prison time that is commensurate with your crimes, I do understand and, to some degree, appreciate your willingness to cooperate, even if you really have little choice. As such, I hereby accept and approve the terms of the cooperation agreement. As part of the agreement, and directly pursuant to your crimes, you will be remanded to the custody of the U.S. marshals who will escort you to a maximum-security penitentiary prison in Florence, Colorado for a period of 132 months. I wish you the best of luck. Godspeed, Mr. Hennessey."

Stu hung his head in shame. All he could think of was the resentment that his father, uncle, and grandfather had upon learning that he wanted to become a federal agent. If they were alive today, that shame would pale in comparison to the dishonor he had brought to himself, his family legacy, and the agency he'd toiled for so many years to serve. He raised his eyes and meekly said, "Thank you, your honor."

Operation Long Arm

A crowd of reporters gathered outside of the Southern District of New York courthouse. Representatives from all the major news networks, and some from the foreign press, had been jostling for a position near the steps of the court since the impromptu press conference was announced. No one knew what it was about, but it promised to be big news. The setting sun over the iconic buildings in lower Manhattan cast shadows perfectly capturing the uneasiness of the crowd. Moments later, the heavy gold-colored doors to the court opened wide as Dre and Richard Ramos, both stone-faced, approached the podium. Dre removed some documents from his inner suit pocket and began to speak.

"Good evening. My name is Andre Carter. I am with the U.S. Attorney's office for the Southern District of New York. Accompanying me is Richard Ramos, Chief Detective of the Federal Bureau of Investigation. Two years ago, Operation Long Arm, was initiated to investigate and infiltrate a nefarious group known as the Order of the Tempest. For years, Tempest has been utilizing a global network to engage in a wide range of criminality, including acts of murder, drug, and human trafficking, tax evasion, campaign finance violations, racketeering, extortion, bribery, and a long list of other crimes. With the assistance of very highly placed and corrupt government, municipal and corporate officials, Tempest has been able to act without impunity."

Cameras snapped frantically as Dre continued. "Numerous agencies have partnered in this massive operation including the FBI's Criminal and White-collar Crime Divisions, DEA, ATF, IRS, and various other federal, state, and local law enforcement officers throughout the United States. The investigation has also been receiving assistance from Interpol and other international law enforcement agencies. Thanks to the stalwart cooperation and dedication of these agencies, we have made great progress in the infiltration of this sinister group and captured some of its members. Indeed, numerous arrests have already been made and our offices have procured cooperating witnesses, whose identities shall remain anonymous for their own protection. We will not rest until we have completely eradicated this criminal syndicate. For far too long, Tempest has acted as if they were above the law. As of today, that all ends."

A reporter attempted to ask a question, but Dre continued, "An investigation into a decades old murder at a psychiatric facility in Rockland County led to a major break in the case. Information from that case helped to fill some of the gaps that were missing for us to infiltrate members of the local Tempest group. However, we need help from the public. To the extent at all possible, our offices will begin sharing information. In particular, we need help in identifying certain individuals who are alleged associates of the Tempest group yet remain at large. We have set up a hotline and website to field any and all leads from the public. I will now take some of your questions."

Legacy

Martin Walcott had just left his attorney's office. He had spent the last twelve hours discussing a legal strategy for his appeal from the disciplinary action he was issued by the ethics committee of the National Board of Pathology for multiple acts of moral turpitude. The Board had received several complaints about his work on prior cases and he now faced permanent expulsion and the dramatic loss of his prized fellowship with this professional organization. He also stood to lose his medical license and faced a multitude of criminal and civil malpractice charges, but for Walcott, his fellowship, in many ways, meant the most to him. It served as the very token of his legacy.

At the preliminary hearing, the complaints came from an anonymous source. The source of this information was withheld from him, but he knew precisely where they came from. Walcott could not fathom how the involvement of a stranger named Savoy Graves and his wife, the couple he so brazenly whisked away not long ago, could have exposed him and led to his professional ruin. A thorough investigation into Walcott's record raised a total of sixteen confirmed counts of misconduct and gross negligence.

When he first received the Board's decision to strip him of his fellowship, Walcott was crushed. He was a pioneer and well-connected member of the medical and business community. His precious legacy that he had worked long and hard to build and maintain was crumbling before his eyes. Yet, deep down, he was not truly surprised by his fall from grace. In fact, he had grown to expect the possibility that his reputation would one day be tarnished, or worse. All it would take, he feared, was one allegation, one mere whiff of foul play among the many cases he had overseen in his career that would lead to another, and so on. The more scrutiny he faced, the more he would be incriminated, likely leading to the downfall of his precious legacy.

Despite his anguish, Walcott had much more to worry about. If Tempest believed that he had brought about unwanted attention to them, then he would surely suffer under their retribution. Walcott has been a member of the group for many years and, like all members, was keenly aware of the dire consequences of falling out of favor with them.

As he approached his car, Walcott fumbled for the keys in his pocket. He pulled them out and nervously scanned the parking lot before gaining entry. He sat with his hands shaking. He had trouble thinking clearly as he wiped his face, now dripping with sweat. He blinked several times before noticing a bright white flower on the car's dashboard. He had first found it placed in the passenger seat of his car this morning and its presence had puzzled him all day. He was riveted by the brilliant white petals shining brightly with the help of the overhead parking lights. He smelled its fresh fragrance before placing it back onto the passenger seat. He then started the car and reached for the gear when Luis, who was hidden in the back seat, sat up, instantly reaching around to place his left hand firmly on Walcott's forehead. With his right hand he drove a sharp blade through the back of his neck, exiting through his mouth, killing him instantly. Luis removed his blade and wiped it on his victim's coat. He then retrieved the flower and plucked one of its petals before quietly exiting the car.

A Gentle Grip

Savoy stood before Loretta as she lay peacefully on her hospital bed, wearing a white gown. Her hairless head was covered by a violet colored knitted cap and her face was contorted with pain. The room was adorned by many bouquets of flowers and smelled of a coconut scented body lotion used to moisturize her hands and feet. The soft music of Chopin's "Raindrop" played gently from a nearby radio in concert with the EKG machine used to monitor her vital signs which were clearly failing. It would not be long now.

Although Savoy promised her that he would do his best at finding out the truth about Adeline's death, he never fooled himself. From start to finish, this was the greatest test of courage and determination that he had ever known. It almost cost him everything. And through it all, he and Lola achieved a level of justice that he never thought possible. And as he held Loretta's soft hand, he only wished that she could hear the results of his findings. He leaned in to whisper in her ear, "Loretta, it's Savoy," he said. "If you can hear me, you were right. Adeline did not kill herself, as they've wrongly said for all these years. I am sorry to say that she was murdered. Her killer is now dead. He was shot while attacking us in our home. Those who were also involved will soon face justice as well. I am so sorry for Adeline. I hope you can hear me and that this gives you some peace before you leave us. When you see Adeline, give her a kiss from us, and ask her if we can call her Addy."

Savoy continued to hold her hand, wishing for a gentle grip, or some sign to acknowledge that she had heard his words. He studied her carefully. Gone was the painful look on her face, and for a fleeting instant, he thought that he had noticed a look, albeit a slight one, of comfort, seconds before the EKG machine flat-lined. Doctors rushed in as Savoy stepped back to allow them to examine her. The look on their faces confirmed the obvious. Moments later, Loretta Deveraux was officially pronounced dead.

As the nurses exited the room, Savoy returned and placed his hand on top of hers to say a brief prayer. He was filled with bittersweet feelings. Although her death saddened him, it was expected, given her condition, and now she was relieved of her chronic pain. More importantly, he believed in his heart that Loretta heard his words just before she died. For so much of her life, this is all she wanted to hear—what she *needed* to hear. He now felt that she could truly rest in peace and this comforted him. Savoy exited the hospital and walked slowly toward his car. Flying high above the parking lot, he could see a pair of cardinals circling overhead. The birds were chirping playfully, almost as if in dance, before disappearing over a patch of trees. He couldn't understand why, but his encounter with these birds gave him great comfort.

Epilogue

Despite Stu's fall from grace, the reality was not lost upon any of them that without his full cooperation, Ramos' team would have had a difficult time infiltrating Tempest. In fact, his cooperation led to a heavy, albeit far from complete, dismantling of the group. The information he provided led to the incrimination and arrest of numerous Tempest operatives, along with several state judges and local law enforcement officials, a dozen corporate CEO's, two music industry moguls, a senior drug trafficker, and a plethora of other mid to low level criminals in a few short years.

While it was never publicly expressed, and despite being despised for his crimes, some within the FBI, including Richard Ramos, felt a strong measure of sympathy and even respect for Stu. To be sure, his betrayal was unforgivable, and he received what he deserved. However, the acceptance of his fate, while exhibiting a true sense of remorse and cooperating zealously with the agency helped change their perception of him, even if only slightly.

Just six years into his prison term, Stu was diagnosed with pancreatic cancer. He died a short time later and was buried in a cemetery in a plot with his father and grandfather in Cyprus Hills, New York. Unlike the tombstones of his proud patriarchs, and in accordance with his final wishes, Stu's tombstone read that he was a dedicated agent of the FBI.

Investigators extracted DNA samples from the body of Doug Reynolds and compared them with the samples preserved in Bonnie's duplicate rape kit taken more than 40 years ago. They were an identical match. This, coupled with his oral admission before he died, confirmed that Doug was responsible for the rape and murder of Adeline Marie Deveraux in 1977 at the Thornwood Manor Psychiatric Center.

Prior to his death, and unbeknownst to Doug, the employees at his meat processing plant in Jamaica, New York had begun an organizing campaign to join a local Teamsters Union. An election was held just two weeks after his death. The employees voted unanimously to join the union and today they enjoy fair wages, favorable working conditions, and dignity in the workplace.

Shannon Hicks sat at her usual table in a coffee shop in Sleepy Hollow, New York, a place she had regularly visited since her retirement. As she waited for her breakfast, she read the local newspaper. On the fourth page, she was stunned to see a story about the death of Adeline

Marie Deveraux. The headline read "Justice delayed, but Never Too Late." In amazement, Shannon read about how the girl's death was falsely labeled a suicide by Martin Walcott who was exiled from the medical industry and now faced a wide array of criminal and civil charges relating to cases he had worked on. His dramatic fall from grace drew a smile upon Shannon's face. "The bastard deserved that," she whispered. The story also detailed how Adeline's killer was discovered, but before being placed under arrest, he was shot and killed after breaking into the house of the man who was investigating the case.

Nearing the end of the article, she read how credit was given to Bonnie Beacham and her mentor, Solomon Vessey, for their efforts in the investigation. Shannon was breathless. She recalled how she and Bonnie toiled in Walcott's office so many years ago and were subjected to cruel harassment and disrespect from their male colleagues. She also recalled how more than forty years ago she'd mailed copies of Bonnie's files to her home. She didn't know it at the time, but Adeline's file was among those she had sent, and it proved to be a catalyst for solving the crime and cover-up. This gave her a great deal of satisfaction. Shannon reached for her cup of coffee and with fond thoughts of her friend Bonnie, she said aloud, "Oorah, my friend. Oorah."

Stanley Korman was questioned by police about his actions leading to the death of Doug Reynolds. His gun was properly registered, and after a thorough investigation, it was concluded that Doug had broken into the home with the full intention of taking the lives of its occupants, and Stanley's actions were proper under the circumstances.

Stanley was more than happy to continue watching his neighbors' dogs as Lola was recovering in the hospital. Two days later, he sat at his kitchen table with his cell phone in hand. He tossed a snack to Clubber and Vito before slowly dialing the number that was written down on a small piece of paper. On the second ring, his daughter, Charlotte, answered the call. After an initial few moments of awkwardness, they spent more than three hours on the call. They each apologized for not taking the time to see more of each other and Stanley even made plans to finally visit his daughter in the coming weeks where he planned to take her up on her offer to give him free sky diving lessons. When he ended the call, Stanley could not contain his smile. It was not at all what he had feared all these years, and he could not believe that he'd waited so long to take Lola's advice.

Bonnie Beacham boarded an afternoon ferry to Connecticut on her way back to her home in Salem. She recalled her mood on her trip to New York. She'd been naturally somber, given the news of the death of her father, but she was burdened by so much more pain. Pain that stemmed from the crushing defeat at the hands of Martin Walcott. She had long felt that his deeds took more than her career; he'd crushed a part of her soul and she had never recovered from that.

On her return trip, however, Bonnie's mood could not be any more to the contrary. Vanessa was due to return home next week, and she could not wait to reconnect with her daughter, whose adventurous tales always brought a smile to her face and a boost to her soul. The results of the last couple of weeks had shed a new light in her life. After all, her efforts, long ago, in Adeline's case played a large part in achieving some measure of justice while implicating Martin Walcott of wrongdoing. These results provided the very validation that was stolen from her long ago. Yes, Walcott had taken so much from her, which can never be recovered, but, for the first time, she realized he could never steal her training, diligence, and professionalism. Most importantly, for the first time, she finally felt that she'd lived up to her part of the bargain with her father. The sun began to set over the Long Island Sound. As the ferry passed a nearby lighthouse, she smiled wildly. She could think of nothing, but her father, and sweet redemption.

One day after watching Dre's press conference at the steps of the Southern District of New York, Jonah Stern called the bookstore and immediately resigned. He was keenly aware of the reputation of Tempest to exact revenge on those who had brought unwanted scrutiny to their fraternal order. Although he played a small part in this case, he would not leave it to chance. That same evening, a clean-shaven Jonah rented a car and began a long journey to visit some friends who lived in Van Buren, Maine. Today, his whereabouts are unknown. However, anyone who knows him can expect Jonah to continue his reading of antiquities, questioning everything and forever watching the skies.

Martin Walcott frequently traveled across the country to attend lectures and fundraisers. Thus, lengthy absences drew no suspicions from his neighbors. On this day, the local mailman arrived to deliver the mail to the homes on his block. When he reached Walcott's home, he was met with an overly stuffed mailbox filled with varying pieces of mail, including utility bills, junk mail, and other solicitations. He pressed down on the bulky pile and placed the one letter to be delivered to the home on the top.

The envelope was addressed to Martin and was sent to him by the

National Board of Pathology. It contained a letter with the results of his appeal: one that he anxiously awaited but would never get to read. The neatly typed letter, signed by Board president Bernadette Johnson stated:

> *Dear, Mr. Walcott:*
>
> *After a thorough review of the evidence on record regarding the above referenced case number, the Board has determined that the evidence irrefutably indicates that you have engaged in multiple counts of moral turpitude. Accordingly, your appeal has been denied and your permanent expulsion from the National Board of Pathology is hereby upheld and your fellowship is permanently revoked.*

The day had finally arrived, and Savoy hurried Lola as they prepared to leave to the hospital. "You don't want to have this baby in the car, do you?" he asked.

Lola smiled while packing her bag and responded, "Relax, labor could take hours."

Her response did nothing to calm his nerves and he continued to hurry her along. As they finally prepared to leave, they stood at the doorway and Lola said, "By the time we return, we will have our little baby with us." This drew a smile on both their faces as they closed the door and entered the car.

They left the home in somewhat of a mess, particularly by Lola's standards, who always worked to keep it in pristine condition—a trait imparted upon Lola by the grandmother who'd raised her. Thus, she always chased after Savoy to pick up after himself. With the baby soon entering their lives, she would not tolerate a messy house and Savoy was more than happy to oblige. However, they had a date with the child who would be entering this world in a few hours, and a messy home is but a small sacrifice for Lola to make.

It was a dream come true for two people who had met during the most difficult of circumstances: Savoy investigating the death of Lola's mother, a woman she had never met. They had also just endured a great deal of emotional and physical strain in the past few months, culminating in the dangerous encounter with Doug whose blade pierced Lola's abdomen nearly killing her and their unborn child. Thankfully, her wounds healed, their spirits were high, and the baby was on the way.

There was an energetic glow throughout the Graves household, which all seemed to emanate from the upstairs bedroom that would soon be occupied by their child. Since Savoy and Lola refused to learn the baby's gender until the birth, they'd painted the room a soft yellow: an agreed upon "neutral" color. The room was bright, airy, and well kept. It had simple white furniture with a changing table. The walls were adorned of pictures of flowers, animals, and other decorative items. There were also pictures of Savoy and Lola, the dogs, and, of course, the picture with Lola's mother, Maria, wearing a beautiful, yet simple, blue dress, taken so long ago while she was pregnant with Lola.

The crib was made of beautiful wood oak and lined with soft blue bedding. A mobile of baby farm animals hung from above, and soft pillows were propped inside. Everything was in order. There was joy in the Graves' household. And there, placed delicately on a soft pillow in the middle of the crib, lay a magnificent pearly white ghost orchid.

ACKNOWLEDGEMENTS

This book is dedicated to my wonderful wife, Migdalia Ortiz-Torres whose spirit, strength, love, and belief in me, along with her much needed critical thinking, careful analysis, and diligent research, has made this project possible.

This book is also dedicated to my children, Isabella, Jake, and Olivia who continue to inspire me every day to be a better father, person, teacher, and writer.

I would specifically like to thank my daughter, Isabella, for her support and strength; my son, Jake, for his technical support and encouragement in this project; and my daughter, Olivia, for the amazing and inspiring artwork used in the cover design.

I would also like to thank my mother, Grace, whose strength knows no bounds; my family, friends, and colleagues for their dedicated and unending support; Vanessa Anderson for her enthusiastic and professional editing and book design services in this project; Peter Speth M.D. for his invaluable medical analysis; David Bertram for his wisdom in law enforcement; and all those who have touched my life, no matter how big or small, lasting or fleeting, in ways that have lent creative inspiration to this book.

FURTHER READING

More information can be found on
Facebook, LinkedIN,
and Twitter @MTorresAuthor1